THE NATURE OF GOD

BY DON HASTINGS AND MARC GIBSON

ONE STONE
BIBLICAL RESOURCES

Published by:
One Stone Press
420 Old Morgantown Rd.
Bowling Green, KY 42101

Printed in the United States of America

ISBN 10: 0-9854938-0-1
ISBN 13: 978-0-9854938-0-6

Supplemental Materials Available:

~ Power Point Slides for each lesson

~ Answer Key

~ Downloadable PDF

www.onestone.com

ONE STONE
BIBLICAL RESOURCES

PREFACE

The study of the nature and character of God is considered by the authors of this workbook as one of utmost important and greatly needed in the church today. There is, perhaps, no greater subject the human mind could contemplate. Every lesson was written with these considerations in mind. Each individual lesson was written by one of the authors of this workbook, and then reviewed by the other. The author of the individual lessons is as follows: Don Hastings – Lessons 1, 3, 4, 7, 8, 11, 13 and Marc Gibson – Lessons 2, 5, 6, 9, 10, 12. We have prepared this workbook in the hope that it contributes to a greater knowledge of our God and Creator, and brings glory to His name.

DON HASTINGS & MARC GIBSON

TABLE OF CONTENTS

KNOW GOD

MAN'S GREATEST NEED IS TO

It is with fear and trembling that we endeavor to understand, to the best of our ability, the awesome nature of God. There is not a higher, more pre-eminent, majestic, sublime subject to challenge our minds! Let us meditate soberly and reverently on the Supreme Being.[1]

How wonderful it is that God has given us the ability to think rationally. He wants us to use this ability to get to know him. God's marvelous creation of the earth and universe declare his glory, wisdom, and power (Psa. 19:1; 104:24; Rom. 1:20). "Who can look at majestic mountains, the beauty of a rising or setting sun, or walk through a flower garden without being impressed with the glory of the Creator?"[2] He has graciously revealed his thoughts and characteristics in the Bible. One can only learn his will for man through a study of the inspired Scriptures. All attempts end in vain when man tries to know the mind and will of God apart from his word.

We must not be like Pharaoh who said, "I do not know the Lord..." (Ex. 5:2).[3] Pharaoh was not afraid of the Lord of slaves. Because he did not know the Lord, he adamantly defied the Lord and suffered severe punishment through the plagues the Lord brought upon him and the Egyptians. He came to know that no earthly power can defeat the awesome power of God!

WHY MAN NEEDS TO KNOW GOD

Man's greatest need is to know the Lord for Jesus said, "And this is life eternal, that they may know You, the only true God, and Jesus Christ whom You have sent" (Jn. 17:3). Eternal life is dependent on an accurate knowledge of God. This knowledge should produce faith in him (Rom. 10:17). One author explained it this way:

The study of God must always be one of the Christian's top priorities, since the knowledge of God is one of the main pillars in a life of piety. When Jesus prayed for his disciples, he said, "And this is eternal life, that they may know Thee, the only true God, and Jesus Christ whom Thou hast sent" (John 17:3). Eternal life depends upon knowing God. This includes knowing about God, but it also includes knowing God existentially and personally. That is, we must make the facts about God determinative for our whole life and thought. We must embrace the truth about God with our whole hearts and mold our lives around it. We must live as though God is truly real; we must take his reality seriously.[4]

Without faith in God "it is impossible to please Him" (Heb. 11:6). God has given us sufficient knowledge of himself to produce complete trust in him (Prov. 16:20). This trust will cause us to obey him which will result in the salvation of our souls (Matt. 7:21). Without the knowledge of God and his righteousness, ignorance becomes a serious danger to our souls (Rom. 10:1-3). One writer commented on the lack of understanding of God even among those who are regular church-goers:

> ...They are engaged in "church activities," given pep talks, how-to-do-it lectures and conversion sermons; they are encouraged to pray to God, to be godly, and to win others to God; they are to give to God, serve God, and desire to see Him and spend eternity with Him; but seldom if ever are they taught anything about Him, His nature and His attributes. It is no wonder that many churches have to give prizes to get people to ride their buses to the church house.[5]

We prove that we know the nature, character, and will of God by our obedience to his commandments. "Now by this we know that we know Him, if we keep His commandments. He who says, 'I know Him,' and does not keep His commandments, is a liar, and the truth is not in him" (1 Jn. 2:3, 4). Do you know God? Are you a faithful worshiper and servant of "the living and true God" (1 Thess. 1:9)?

If we fail to acquire a true knowledge of God, we will suffer horrible punishment! When Jesus comes again, he will come "with His mighty angels, in flaming fire taking vengeance on those who do not know God, and on those who do not obey the gospel of our Lord Jesus Christ. These shall be punished with everlasting destruction from the presence of the Lord and from the glory of His power" (2 Thess. 1:7-9). In the judgment, one will not be excused for his failure to obey God because of his ignorance of God.

KNOWING GOD THROUGH JESUS

We can learn much about the nature of God by studying the life and teaching of Jesus, the Son of God. "Philip said to Him, 'Lord, show us the Father, and it is sufficient for us.'" Jesus answered, "He who seen Me has seen the Father" (Jn. 14:8, 9). To know Jesus is to know the Father. Jesus was "Immanuel" which means, "God with us" (Matt. 1:23).

In the New Testament, we can see Jesus as He lived on earth. As we see Him reacting to circumstances, as we see His tears, as we hear His groaning, as we witness flashes of anger at the evil conduct of men, as we hear Him condemn the hypocrisies of the Pharisees and preach the Sermon on the Mount, as we view His walk from Gethsemane to the cross, and as we hear Him commission the apostles to "go into all the world and preach the gospel to every creature," we are seeing and hearing God![6]

We should be very thankful that the Father has revealed himself through his Son (Heb. 1:1-3). There is no better way for God to have revealed himself to mankind than for his Son to put on a body of flesh and live among men (Phil. 2:7).

CAN THE FINITE UNDERSTAND THE INFINITE?

The word, "finite," means, "Having bounds, ends, or limits, as opposed to that which is infinite."[7] The word "infinite" means, "So great as to be immeasurable and unbounded; limitless...."[8] Man is finite, but God is infinite. While God has made us capable of understanding to a degree some of his attributes, it is impossible for us to fully fathom them. We would have to be on equality with God to do that. "The finite cannot comprehend the infinite; the time-bound cannot imagine the time-less."[9] God has neither beginning nor end of existence.

"Have you not known? Have you not heard? The everlasting God, the Lord, the Creator of the ends of the earth, neither faints nor is weary. There is no searching of His understanding" (Isa. 40:28). "Oh, the depth of the riches both of the wisdom and knowledge of God! How unsearchable are His judgments and His ways past finding out! 'For who has known the mind of the Lord? Or who has become His counselor?' 'Or who has first given to Him and it shall be repaid to him?' For of Him and through Him and to Him are all things, to whom be glory forever. Amen" (Rom. 11:33-

36). The love of Christ "passes knowledge" (Eph. 3:19). The peace of God "surpasses all understanding" (Phil. 4:7).

"We cannot completely define God, because we cannot completely understand God. This does not mean that we cannot have any knowledge of God, nor does it mean that we cannot grow in our understanding of the divine revelation. But it does mean that our conception of God must be limited, for man is the finite being and God is the infinite being."[10] We should not be discouraged over our inability to answer many questions about God's divine nature. "The secret things belong to the Lord our God, but those things which are revealed belong to us and to our children forever, that we may do all the words of this law" (Deut. 29:29). We should rejoice over the information God has seen fit to make known about himself and be eager to absorb this knowledge. Our inability to answer some questions about God does not mean that he does not exist. We do not understand all there is to know about the human body, but that fact does not mean that it does not exist.

WHAT WE WOULD NOT KNOW WITHOUT KNOWING GOD

Without knowledge of God, there are many wonderful truths that we would not know. We would be ignorant of how we came to exist on earth for we would not know that God created us in his image and from the "dust of the ground" (Gen. 1:26, 27; 2:7). The unreasonable theory of evolution is man's desperate attempt to explain his existence apart from God. Such denials of God and the supernatural (atheism, secular humanism) result in man being lost in his ignorance.

We would not know that our purpose on earth is to "fear God and keep His commandments" (Eccl. 12:13). We would be hopelessly lost as sheep without a shepherd for we would not know the "good shepherd" who cares for us and leads us to eternal life (Jn. 10:11, 27-28).

We would have no absolute standard of right and wrong or truth and error (Jn. 17:17). Man's fallible, fickle mind is constantly changing his moral standard to justify his immoral desires. This is easily seen in how the ethical standard has changed in our lifetime. Some examples are homosexuality, divorce, men and women living together without being married to each other, etc. Man removes laws he does not like and enacts laws that permit him to do legally things which were once forbidden. "O Lord, I know the way of man is not in himself; it is not in man who walks to direct his own steps" (Jer. 10:23).

We would not know of his immeasurable love for us which was demonstrated by sending his Son to die for us (Jn. 3:16). We would not know what is sinful and that sin has separated us from God's fellowship (Isa. 59:2). We would be ignorant of the truth that only Christ's blood can wash away our sins in baptism so we may be reconciled with God (Matt. 26:28; Acts 22:16; 2 Cor. 5:18-21).

What a horrible tragedy to live "having no hope and without God in the world" (Eph. 2:12)! Those who willfully live in ignorance of God can only view themselves as a piece of matter that exists for a brief moment and then eternal darkness. "The wicked in his proud countenance does not seek God; God is in none of his thoughts" (Psa. 10:4; cf. Rom. 3:11). Let us take up the challenge to know our God – it is our greatest need!

QUESTIONS

1. What is man's greatest need? _To Know the Lord._

2. What is the best way we can use our ability to reason? _____

3. What does God's marvelous creation reveal about him? _It declares his glory wisdom and power_ _____ (give scriptures) _Psa 19:1, 104:24, Rom 1:20_

4. Where is the only place to learn about God's will for us? _____

5. On what is eternal life dependent? (give scripture) _Eternal life is dependent on an accurate knowledge of God   John 17:3, Romans 10:17_

6. What does "Immanuel" mean? _God with us_

7. Can one fully understand God's attributes? Explain. _No, in order to do so we would be equal, and infinite, but we are not._

8. Why should we not be discouraged that our knowledge of God is limited? _____

FILL IN THE BLANK

1. A knowledge of God should produce _faith_ in him.

2. To _Know_ Jesus is to _Know_ the Father.

3. To completely understand God's nature, we would have to be _Infinite_.

4. Man is finite, but God is _infinite_.

GIVE BOOK, CHAPTER, AND VERSE

1. "There is no searching of His understanding" _Isa 40:28_

2. "How unsearchable are His judgments" _Romans 11: 33_

3. The love of Christ "passes knowledge" _Eph 3:19_

4. The peace of God "surpasses all understanding" _Phil 4:7_

5. "Fear God and keep His commandments" _Eccl 12:13_

WITHOUT A KNOWLEDGE OF GOD, WE WOULD NOT KNOW:

1. How we came to _exist_ and our _purpose_ on earth.

2. The absolute _Standard_ of _right_ and _wrong_.

3. God's immeasurable _Love_ for us and his plan of _Salvation_.

THOUGHT QUESTIONS

1. Do you know the Lord? Explain how you came to know the Lord.

2. Define "finite" and "infinite."

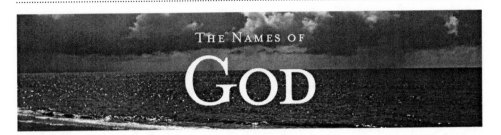

The Names of GOD

Names are important things. Parents usually give a great deal of thought to naming their children. We use our names throughout our lives to identify ourselves, even to the very end on our grave markers.

The importance of a name is illustrated in the very beginning when "the Lord God formed every beast of the field and every bird of the air, and brought them to Adam to see what he would call them. And whatever Adam called each living creature, that was its name" (Gen. 2:19). "This association of the act of naming with creation underlines the fact that the name represents something wholesome and salutary; the knowledge of the name opens up specific human dimensions for communication and for fellowship."[1]

In the Hebrew Old Testament, the use of names often carried meanings associated with the one who had that name. God changed Abram's name to Abraham (Gen. 17:5). The name, Abraham, means "father of a multitude."[2] God changed Sarai, the wife of Abraham, to Sarah (Gen. 17:15). The name Sarah, means "princess."[3] Jesus said that Simon "'shall be called Cephas' (which is translated, A Stone)" (Jn. 1:42). Our modern practice of naming is quite different.

In English, names are usually chosen for such reasons as having been in the family previously, the way they sound in themselves or in combination with the surname, or due to some parental whim. Any meaning of a name is generally unknown and irrelevant in its choice. Hebrew names, on the other hand, are readily "readable" by those who hear or see them: David means "beloved"; Nabal, "fool"; and Ishbaal, "man of the lord." They can actually carry some meaning instead of just being an arbitrary symbol for the one who bears them.[4]

A HOLY AND REVEREND NAME

The Psalmist wrote, "Holy and awesome (reverend, KJV) is His name" (Psa. 111:9b). God's people are to "fear this glorious and awesome name" (Deut. 28:58). This is why God's name must never be "taken in vain" (Ex. 20:7). When an "Israelite woman's son blasphemed the name of the Lord and cursed," the Lord said, "...let all the congregation stone him...And whoever blasphemes the name of the Lord shall surely be put to death, and all the congregation shall surely stone him, the stranger as well as him who is born in the land. When he blasphemes the name of the Lord, he shall be put to death" (Lev. 24:11-16). This Old Testament event should cause us to realize how much God abhors hearing his holy name blasphemed. However, many are guilty of blaspheming his exalted name. Such vain and blasphemous usage of God's name involves an irreverent use of a holy name that drags it below a common level and puts it in a position to be ridiculed and mocked. Also, false swearing by God's name and profaning (polluting) his names are prohibited (Lev. 19:12; 18:21).

The one God is known by different designations in the Scriptures, and "the Old Testament contains a number of names and compound names for God which reveal Him in some aspect of His character and dealings with mankind."[5] It is essential for man to know and understand the names that God has revealed for himself which speak to his character, nature, and position of glory and honor. Moses, when he stood before the burning bush, was concerned that he identify God properly to the children of Israel: "Then Moses said to God, 'Indeed, when I come to the children of Israel and say to them, "The God of your fathers has sent me to you," and they say to me, "What is His name?" what shall I say to them?'" (Ex. 3:13). We should be just as concerned that we understand and properly use the names of God.

THREE MAJOR NAMES FOR GOD

Three major names are used for God in the Old Testament:

ELOHIM

Elohim is the name used in the first verse of the Bible: "In the beginning God [*elohim*] created the heavens and the earth" (Gen. 1:1). This frequently used name is a plural form of the singular *Eloah*. They are both related to the more general form, *El*, and are the most common designations for deity in ancient Semitic languages. This name of God "probably derives from a root meaning 'power' or 'preeminence.'"[6] *Elohim* is especially descriptive of God's power in his creative works and preservation of all things. It can also refer to the false pagan deities (Ex. 20:3; 32:1; Psa. 95:3), and even human judges of Israel (Psa. 82:1, 6).

> This plural word also reveals the plurality of persons sharing the essence of deity. Robert B. Girdlestone explains that "there is certainly nothing unreasonable in the supposition that the name of the Deity was given to man in this form, so as to prepare him for the truth that in the unity of the Godhead there are Three Persons."[7] Some see it only as a "plural of majesty" or a "royal plural," but it must be noted that plural pronouns are used with it in Genesis 1:26 – "Then God [*Elohim*] said, 'Let Us make man in Our image, according to Our likeness...'". The true *Elohim* is one God (deity, Deut. 6:4), but encompasses three personalities, which later would be revealed as the triune Father, Son [Word, Jn. 1:1], and Holy Spirit (Matt. 28:19).[8]

YAHWEH

This name was written originally as the tetragrammaton YHWH.[9] Its original pronunciation is unknown, and Jewish tradition was to speak the word *adonay* in its place so as to not take this important name in vain. Sadly, most today have no fear of speaking God's holy name in vain! It is at the burning bush that Moses heard God give his name as "I AM" (Ex. 3:14). It is believed that *Yahweh* is derived from the Hebrew verb *havah* meaning "to be, being." Man began to call upon this name early in human history, and it was known and used by the patriarchs (Gen. 4:26; 14:22; 15:18).[10]

Yahweh is the most commonly used name (over 6800 times), expressing God's eternal existence and becoming a special name involved in God's covenant relationship with the nation of Israel (Ex. 3:15; 6:7; 20:2). "Yahweh is the only truly personal name of God in Israel's faith; the others are titular or descriptive expressions. References to 'the name' or 'in the name' of God indicate this name."[11] *Elohim* and *Yahweh* are used together in such passages as 2 Chron. 14:11, and in Psalms 19 (vv. 1-6 *Elohim*; vv. 7-14 *Yahweh*). In older English versions, "Jehovah" is used, formed by a Latinized combination using the consonants of *Yahweh* and the vowels for *adonay*.[12] Shortened forms of *Yahweh* are found in terms such as "hallelujah" (Praise Yah) and names such as "Elijah" (Yah is God).

ADONAY

Adonay was a common term for lord, or master (Mal. 1:6; human masters – Gen. 18:12; 1 Sam. 26:19; Ex. 21:5). It indicates authority, right to act or speak, preeminence. It is translated as "Lord" (see Gen. 15:2; Ex. 34:23; Deut. 10:17; Josh. 3:11; Judg. 16:28; Psa. 110:1).[13] It occurs frequently with the name *Yahweh*.

> This name reminds us of our need to submit to God's authority. "As our Lord, He has the right to command and we have the responsibility to obey. If we can understand the role of civil authorities and employers over us, we should certainly be able to comprehend the right of God to command us."[14]

Old Testament passages using all three of the above names for God are quoted in the New Testament and applied to Jesus demonstrating that He is God (deity).[15]

> **Elohim** [Gk. *theos*] – Heb. 1:8-9
> **Yahweh** [Gk. *kurios*] – Heb. 1:10; Jn. 8:58
> **Adonay** [Gk. *kurios*] – Matt. 22:43-44

OTHER NAMES AND DESCRIPTIONS OF GOD

El Shaddai (Almighty God)

Gen. 17:1; 28:3; 35:11; 43:14; 48:3; 49:25
Was the name most known and used by the patriarchs (Ex. 6:3)

El Elyon (God Most High)

Gen. 14:18, 22; Num. 24:16; Dan. 7:18, 22, 25, 27
Psalm 91:1-2 – "He who dwells in the secret place of the Most High (*elyon*) shall abide under the shadow of the Almighty (*shaddai*). I will say of the Lord (*yahweh*), 'He is my refuge and my fortress; my God (*elohim*), in Him I will trust."

El Olam (Everlasting God)

Gen. 21:33; Isa. 40:28; cf. Psa. 90:2
Idea also expressed in the phrase "living God" (Josh. 3:10; Psa. 42:2; 84:2; Hos. 1:10)
"Everlasting" is also descriptive of God's love (Jer. 31:3), kindness/mercy (Psa. 100:5; Isa. 54:8), glory (Psa. 104:31), and ways (Hab. 3:6).

El Roi (God Who Sees)

Gen. 16:13

Yahweh Saboath (Lord of Hosts)
1 Sam. 1:3; 2 Sam. 7:27
The Lord of the heavenly hosts (angels) used to accomplish his will and defeat evil.

Abir (Mighty One); Pahad (Fear)
"Mighty God of Jacob" (Gen. 49:24; Psa. 132:2, 5; Isa. 49:26; 60:16)
"Fear of Isaac" (Gen. 31:42, 53)

Greek Names
Theos – "God" (Jn. 1:1; Acts 5:4)
Kurios – "Lord" (Lk. 6:46; 1 Cor. 8:6)

The names attributed to God reveal his character, might, and prominence. Let us be diligent to reflect upon and learn of God from his names, and reverently use them in praise of him. "O LORD, our Lord, how excellent is Your name in all the earth, You who set Your glory above the heavens!" (Psa. 8:1, 9).

QUESTIONS

1. What act soon after the creation illustrated the importance of a name? *The name represents something wholesome and salutary; the knowledge of the name opens up specific human dimensions for communication and for fellowship.*

2. How does the practice of naming someone differ today from that of Old Testament times? _____
_____
_____

3. What does it mean to take God's name in vain? _____
_____
_____

4. Why must we never take God's name in vain? _____
_____
_____
_____

5. What are the three major names for God in the Old Testament?
_____, _____, _____

6. What is the basic word for deity in the ancient Semitic languages, and what is its root meaning? _____

_____

_____

7. Is *Elohim* a singular or plural word? _____ What does this teach about God as revealed in Genesis 1:26? _____

_____

_____

8. What is the most commonly used name for God in the Old Testament?

_____

_____

9. At what occasion did God tell his "name" to Moses? Give scripture.

_____

What did it mean? _____

_____

_____

10. Why does Jewish tradition require speaking another word in place of *Yahweh*? _____

_____

11. Why is *Yahweh* a special name for God? _____

_____

12. How did the word "Jehovah" originate? _____

_____

_____

13. What is the meaning of *adonay*? _____

_____

_____

14. Of the three major names for God in the Old Testament, how many are applied to Jesus in the New Testament quotations? _____

_____

_____

_____

COMPLETE THE SCRIPTURE

1. "Holy and _____ is His name" (Psa. 111:9b).

2. "You shall not take the _____ of the Lord your God in _____, for the Lord will not hold him _____ who takes His name in _____" (Ex. 20:7).

3. "Then God said, 'Let _____ make man in _____ image, according to _____ likeness...'" (Gen. 1:26a).

4. "O Lord, our Lord, how _____ is Your _____ in all the earth, You who set Your _____ above the heavens!" (Psa. 8:1).

MATCH NAME WITH MEANING

1. ___ El Roi
2. ___ El Elyon
3. ___ Theos
4. ___ Pahad
5. ___ El Shaddai
6. ___ Yahweh Saboath
7. ___ Kurios
8. ___ Abir
9. ___ El Olam

a. Almighty God
b. Lord of Hosts
c. God Who Sees
d. Everlasting God
e. Mighty One
f. God
g. God Most High
h. Lord
i. Fear

THOUGHT QUESTIONS

1. Is it scriptural for a man or woman to wear a name or title as "Reverend _____"? Why or why not?

2. Why do you think it is important to know and understand these names of God, even though they were spoken and used long ago in Old Testament times?

God Is The ETERNAL CREATOR (I)

"In the beginning God created the heavens and the earth" (Gen. 1:1). What a majestic declaration that God is the Creator of the universe!

> ...The idea that God is the Creator of all things is the indispensable foundation on which the other beliefs of the Christian faith are based. It affirms what the Christian believes about the status of God in the whole realm of reality: He is the Creator of everything else. On this affirmation logically depends all that Christians say about God, about the world they live in, and about their own history, destiny, and hope.[1]

Many deny this astounding truth. The atheist denies the existence of God. The agnostic believes that God's existence cannot be proved or disproved. In these lessons, we will show that it is more reasonable to believe that God created the heavens, earth, plant and animal life than to believe in the theory of evolution as the cause of the existence of the universe and life.

In the Beginning

The Bible begins with God who has life and mind (1 Thess. 1:9; Rom. 11:34; Acts 14:15).

> So in "the beginning" God already was. Hence, "the beginning" of Genesis 1:1 is the beginning of the material universe, but before that "beginning" there was God! God is the first Cause that caused everything else. Acknowledge this sublime truth and everything else falls into place; deny it and nothing makes sense, including our very existence. That which creates, of necessity, must come before the creation.[2]

The Hebrew word *bara* is translated "create" in Genesis 1:1. "This verb is of profound theological significance, since it has only God as its subject. Only God can 'create' in the sense implied by *bara*."[3] God created the heavens and earth *ex nihilo* (out of nothing) by simply speaking it into existence: "For He spoke, and it was done; He commanded, and it stood fast" (Psa. 33:9; cf. 2 Pet. 3:5). "The creative act of God...involved no preexisting material; a sovereign, all-powerful God created the heavens and the earth from nothing."[4] It is "by faith we understand that the worlds were framed by the word of God, so that the things which are seen were not made of things which are visible" (Heb. 11:3). The creation of heavens, earth, mature plants and animals was an awesome miracle! The power and eternal nature of God are demonstrated by His work of creation, being the great uncaused Cause of all things.

THE DAYS OF CREATION (GENESIS 1)

First Day – God created light and "divided the light from the darkness." He "called the light Day and the darkness He called Night."

Second Day – God made the "firmament," the expanse, or sky. "God called the firmament Heaven."[6]

Third Day – God caused the dry land to appear which he called "Earth" and the waters he called "Seas." He caused the earth to bring forth plant life and said that the seeds from the plants and fruit trees would produce "according to its kind." This law is still in force.

Fourth Day – God made the sun "to rule the day" and the moon "to rule the night." He made so many stars that man is unable to count all of them. "As the host of heaven cannot be numbered, nor the sand of the sea measured..." (Jer. 33:22). At first, man thought he could count all the stars, but now he knows that is impossible.

> Gradually, through the invention of better instruments, the number grew till there is now numbered one hundred billion suns in our galaxy and there is estimated to be trillions of galaxies of which ours is average. To comprehend the possibility of counting stars, if a man were to count the suns just in our Milky Way Galaxy at the rate of 200 per minute, it would take him 1,000 years.[7]

God can not only count the number of stars, but calls them by name. "He counts the number of stars; He calls them all by name. Great is our Lord, and mighty in power; His understanding is infinite" (Psa. 147:4-5).

Fifth Day – God created "an abundance of living creatures" to live in water. He created "every winged bird." He decreed that all animals should reproduce "according to its kind." This law is still in force.

Sixth Day – God created the land animals. He crowned his creative work by creating man and woman "in His own image." Being made in God's image distinguishes man from the other animals for he is an immortal spiritual being. God gave man "dominion" over plant and animal life. They were made for man's benefit.

Genesis 1 gives a general account of the entirety of God's creation. Genesis 2 gives a specific, focused account of the creation of man and woman. There is not a contradiction between the two accounts.[8]

GREAT WISDOM IN GOD'S CREATION

One can easily see God's wisdom in the order of his creation. He created water, light, and dry land before creating plant life. All of these are necessary for plants to live. He created plants before making herbivorous animals. He made plants for man to eat before making man. He created plants, animals and man full grown and capable of reproducing "according to its kind."

How awesome is the wisdom and power of the Creator "who made the world and everything in it" (Acts 17:24)! "O Lord, how manifold are Your works! In wisdom You have made them all" (Psa. 104:24). "By the word of the Lord the heavens were made, and all the host of them by the breath of His mouth. He gathers the waters of the sea together as a heap; He lays up the deep in storehouses. Let all the earth fear the Lord; let all the inhabitants of the world stand in awe of Him. For He spoke, and it was done; He commanded, and it stood fast" (Psa. 33:6-9).

GOD CREATED EVERYTHING "VERY GOOD"

Six times it is recorded in Genesis 1, "God saw that it was good" (vv. 4, 10, 12, 17, 21, 25). The last verse in Genesis 1 states, "Then God saw everything that He had made, and indeed it was very good." He did not need an instruction manual on how, and what, to create. He did not create by trial and error. Perfection and completeness are marks of divine creation.

GOD CREATED THE HEAVENS AND EARTH IN SIX DAYS

"For in six days the Lord made the heavens and the earth, the sea, and all that is in them, and rested on the seventh day" (Ex. 20:11). Each creative day consisted of "evening and morning" (Gen. 1:5, 8, 13, 19, 23, 31). Each day consisted of twenty-four hours. Each day was not millions of years in length as some erroneously argue. If each "evening" was millions of years in length, then all life would have frozen. If each "morning" was millions of years in length, then all life would have burned up. Many plants are dependent on animals for pollination so that they can reproduce. How could they exist for millions of years before animals existed?[9]

> The repetition of "evening and morning" indicates an ordinary 24 hour day. Elsewhere in the Bible the reference seems to be to ordinary days. The six days of creation and the day of God's rest serve as the basis for the Old Testament teaching of working six days and resting on the Sabbath (Ex. 20:11).[10]

THE EARTH AND SUN REVEAL GOD'S INTELLIGENT DESIGN

At 93 million miles away, the sun (which is an average-sized star) is just the right distance from the earth for plant and animal life to exist. If the sun were closer, it would be too hot for life to exist and if it were farther away, it would be too cold for life to exist. "A star is a miracle just as it is. Here is a furnace made of its own fuel, which can run for billions of years without a significant change. Our Sun is a very special kind of star. A star much different than our Sun in size, temperature, rotation rate, or mass could not support a planet Earth."[11] Do you think it is just by chance the sun's temperature, distance, size, rotation rate, and mass are just right for life on earth?

The earth makes an annual revolution around the sun of more than 292 million miles. It is traveling at an estimated speed through space at 70 thousand miles per hour. It takes one year for the earth to make its annual revolution. The word "year" is defined, "The period of time the earth completes a revolution around the sun...365 days, 5 hours, 48 minutes, 46 seconds."[12] To take care of the extra time above 365 days, we have leap year every fourth year. The earth has been making this complete revolution for thousands of years and is never off a second. What amazing precision! The heavenly bodies move with such precision that astronomers know exactly when the next solar eclipse will occur.

The earth spins about 1,000 miles per hour. It would adversely affect our life if it spun 100 miles per hour making our days and nights ten times as long.

The moon is about 240,000 miles from earth. It is the right distance and size for its gravitational force on the earth. The gravitational force between two objects depends on their mass and the distance between them. The gravitational force of the moon affects the ocean tides. The tides might cause the oceans to completely cover all land area if the moon were larger, or closer, to the earth.[13]

There are many other factors absolutely necessary for the existence of life on earth. It has been proven mathematically impossible for all of them to happen by chance.[14]

WHERE THERE IS DESIGN THERE MUST BE A DESIGNER

One would not believe that a house: 1. just naturally evolved over time; 2. was built by a hurricane or volcano eruption; or 3. was built by animals. The only reasonable explanation is that human intelligence built it. "For every house is built by someone, but He who built all things is God" (Heb. 3:4). Since all believe the first half of this verse, why do not all accept the truth of the second half? The building of the universe is extremely more complicated than the building of any house.

There is a story which dates back to the time when the statesman Benjamin Franklin was ambassador of the United States to France. While living in Paris Franklin was a member of the elite literary social and scientific club. At certain of the meetings of this intellectual group, atheistic sentiments were expressed, leaving the impression that only the superstitious and uninformed still believed in God as the creator of the universe. At the next meeting of the group Benjamin Franklin brought a beautifully designed and executed model of the sun and our entire solar system. The earth and the other planets were in their proper relationship to the sun and to each other and of appropriate sizes. It was a masterpiece. Upon seeing it, one of the sophisticated members of the club asked, "Who made it?" Dryly, without a trace of a smile, Franklin responded, "No one. It just happened."[15]

Man can look at a model of our solar system and know that human intelligence must have made it. There is no other reasonable explanation.

However, he looks at this vast, orderly solar system through a telescope and boldly claims that it came into existence through unintelligent matter acting upon itself. How extremely foolish!

There is amazing design in plants, animals, and the very complex human body. Man is still discovering how his marvelous body functions, which God formed from "the dust of the ground" (Gen. 2:7). How can one see this wonderfully designed universe, plant, animal, and human life and conclude that there is not an Intelligent Designer? Truly, none are so blind as those who will not see!

QUESTIONS

1. Write Genesis 1:1 from memory. _____

_____

2. "The beginning" of Genesis 1:1 refers to the beginning of what? _____
   *material beginning*_____

3. What is the significance of the word "create" in Genesis 1:1? _____

_____

_____

4. What distinguishes men and women from animals? (give scripture) ____

_____

_____

_____

5. How may God's wisdom be seen in the *order* of creation? _____

_____

_____

_____

6. How long was each creative day? *24 literal hours*_____

_____

_____

7. What are some theories that deny the literal, consecutive, and sequential creation days? _____

_____

8. How long is one year? _365 days 5 hours, 48 minutes, 46 seconds_

FILL IN THE BLANK

1. God created everything _out_ of _nothing_.

2. God gave man _dominion_ over the animals.

3. "In _wisdom_ You have made them _all_" (give scripture _Psa 104:24_)

4. _Perfection_ and _completeness_ are marks of divine creation.

5. Every created day consisted of "_evening_ and _morning_."

6. The sun's _distance_ and _size_ are just right for _life_ on earth.

7. Where there is _design_ there must be a _designer_.

8. "For every _house_ is built by _someone_, but _He_ who built _all_ things is _God_" (give scripture _Heb 3:4_)

MATCH THE CORRECT DAY OF CREATION

1. _C_ God created plant life   a. 1st Day
2. _D_ God made the sun, moon, and stars   b. 2nd Day
3. _A_ God said, "Let there be light"   c. 3rd Day
4. _F_ God created land animals, man, and woman   d. 4th Day
5. _E_ God created "sea creatures" and birds   e. 5th Day
6. _B_ "God called the firmament Heaven"   f. 6th Day

MULTIPLE CHOICE (CIRCLE THE CORRECT ANSWER)

1. A house must be made by:
   a. Evolution   b. Hurricane   c. Animals   (d.) Humans

2. A model of our solar system must be made by:
   a. Evolution   b. Hurricane   c. Animals   (d.) Humans

3. The solar system must have been made by:
   a. Forces of nature acting on matter   b. Animals   c. Humans   (d.) God

THOUGHT QUESTIONS

1. Give at least two reasons why you believe God is the Eternal Creator.

2. Why is it so critical to defend the literal, historical record of God's creation in Genesis 1?

GOD IS THE
ETERNAL CREATOR (II)

An axiom is "a self-evident or universally accepted truth."[1] There are axioms which state, "Out of nothing comes nothing" and "Something is therefore something was." Since the universe, plant, and animal life exist, then something must be eternal. The only two choices are eternal, lifeless matter (evolution) or eternal intelligence (God). Which one is more reasonable to believe? Does the evidence support God as the uncaused First Cause or does it support inorganic matter? Either choice must be accepted by faith (Heb. 11:3).

> Everyone must admit that something has always existed; and that this something was self-existent, and uncaused. The self-existent is the cause of the world and of life. There has always been something, for something now exists. If at one time there was not anything there would not be anything now. Out of nothing comes nothing. If there were nothing to begin with, there would be nothing to end with. And thus it is that the atheist grants sooner or later that something has always existed and that something was self-existent, uncaused.[2]

WHO MADE GOD?

The atheist asks, "Who made God?" The answer, "No one made God for he has no beginning." The atheist thinks that is a foolish, unreasonable answer. However, the Christian should not be embarrassed about this answer. He should ask the atheist, "How did matter originate?" "How did the universe and life on earth come into existence?" In an effort to answer these important questions, atheists have formulated several theories.

THE BIG BANG THEORY

Of all the theories science has come up with over man's history to explain how the creation came to be, certainly the one known as the "big bang" theory is the best man has been able to invent. It does not solve the problem of the creation itself because it assumes that the matter already existed and that the previously existent primeval mass exploded to produce the cosmos as we see it.[3]

What caused this matter to explode? Was it gases? If the answer is "yes," then ask, "How did these gases originate?" All of these things evolutionists must accept by faith.

Is it reasonable to believe that out of this disorder (explosion) came an orderly universe with trillions of galaxies and each galaxy with about one hundred billion stars? Is it reasonable to believe that lifeless matter produced life? It is more reasonable to believe that an explosion in a print shop produced a dictionary than to believe that inanimate matter exploding made this amazing, orderly universe and produced life.

DEFINITION OF EVOLUTION

Evolution is defined, "Biol. a The doctrine that all forms of life originated by decent, with gradual or abrupt modifications, from preexisting forms which themselves trace backward in a continuing series to the most rudimentary organisms."[4]

By evolution they mean the theory that non-living matter became alive, that this original living matter was simple in its organization, and that the world of living things known today, including man, gradually developed from these original simple forms.[5]

The evolutionary theory is accepted by atheists, and others, as the way by which non-living matter evolved into plant life and plant life evolved into animal life over millions of years. This is the best theory available for one who does not believe there is an Intelligent Creator "who made the world and everything in it" (Acts 17:24).

THE "GENERAL THEORY" AND "SPECIAL THEORY" OF EVOLUTION

Macroevolution, or the "general theory" of evolution, attempts to explain the origin of all plant life coming from non-living matter and that plant life evolved into animal life. Microevolution, or the "special theory" of evolution, states that limited changes take place within "kinds" of plants and animals.

Microevolution is an established fact and does not conflict with what God said about an animal reproducing "according to its kind" (Gen. 1:21, 24, 25). An example of microevolution is that some small horses have evolved into larger horses. However, they are still horses. Another example is that new breeds of dogs have been produced by mating different breeds of dogs. However, they are still dogs. One should not conclude that because there are changes within "kinds" that this is proof one "kind" of animal evolved into another "kind" of animal. Microevolution does not prove macroevolution. Do not be deceived by this unproven argument.

MISSING LINK

Evolutionists speak of the "missing link" as if there is only one missing link. That is not true:

> Anthony Standen, Scientist, in the book, *Science Is A Sacred Cow*, says of the phrase "missing link": "It is a most misleading phrase, because it suggests that only one link is missing. It would be more accurate to say that the greater part of the entire chain is missing, so much that it is not entirely certain whether there is a chain at all" (p. 106).[6]

Fossils revealing undisputed transitional forms of one kind of animal evolving into another kind of animal have *not* been found. If evolution were true, museums should be overflowing with all manner of intermediate, transitional fossils. Their absence speaks volumes about the utter lack of evidence for evolution. Instead, we have a very few claimed transitional fossils which turn out to be distinct species, or worse, frauds.[7]

One of the major predictions of creation is that there was a "sudden appearance of basic plant and animal types without evidence of transitional forms between these basic types."[8] This is exactly what the fossil record reveals, just as it reveals that there was an "abrupt appearance of a great variety of highly complex forms of life" with no evolutionary ancestors found anywhere on earth for these animals.[9] "The historical, or fossil, record thus provides excellent support for special creation, but contradicts the major predictions of evolution theory. In answer to the question, did evolution really occur, the fossils shout a resounding NO!"[10]

SCIENCE IS NOT ABLE TO DISCOVER HOW THE UNIVERSE AND LIFE ORIGINATED

Many scientists, professors, television programs, etc. dogmatically state that evolution has been proven by science to be a fact. However, the evolutionary theory is outside the realm of the scientific method as well as the question of how God created the universe and all life out of nothing.

> The scientific method requires that the experiment be (1) *observable* and 2) *repeatable*. Creation was not observed by any human and is certainly not repeatable. This is not to say that the account of creation is not in harmony with known scientific facts; it simply is not to be judged by scientific criteria.[11]

> Scientists generally acknowledge that they do not know absolutely how the universe and life originated. The whole realm of science is the study of things as they are. Science can examine and analyze present processes and materials but science is not in a position to say how things actually came into existence. Its observations necessarily were begun long after the beginning of the universe. Scientists can make intelligent guesses and offer hypotheses, but they are not in a position to speak with the same authority about how the universe began as they are to speak about the present operation of the universe. A number of prominent men of science have made this distinction quite clear.[12]

Any study of the origins of life and the universe will involve the interpretation of evidence and events based on philosophical presuppositions. Naturalistic evolution denies that there is a God, while biblical creationism accepts God as the Creator. Unless this difference is resolved, the evidence (which is the same for both) will be interpreted in two very different ways. The scientific method cannot resolve this difference. Therefore, it is wrong to say that evolution is entirely scientific and creationism is wholly religious. Both are explanations of origins whose interpretations must be examined in light of the evidence. Unfortunately, evolution itself has become a religious dogma today among those who accept *naturalism* (there is nothing beyond this natural world) in the scientific and educational community, while scientists, educators, and students who believe in God and biblical creation endure unjust discrimination and ridicule.

SCIENTIFIC FACTS AGREE WITH THE BIBLE

"Lord Kelvin, the great British thermodynamicist, once said, 'If you study science deeply enough and long enough it will eventually convince you there is a God.'"[13] Since God's word is truth, it does not contradict what science has proven to be true (Jn. 17:17).[14] The Bible does contradict the fallible theories of man concerning the origin of the universe and life.

Science confirms that the doctrine of biogenesis is a fact. Biogenesis is defined, "The doctrine that life is generated from living organisms only."[15] Evolution contradicts this scientific fact by teaching that plant life originated from non-living matter. Science has never proven that to be true. The living God creating plant and animal life agrees with this doctrine (Gen. 1:11, 20-27; 1 Thess. 1:9; Acts 17:25).

The First and Second Laws of Thermodynamics also agree with the creation model of creation. The First Law of Thermodynamics, or the principle of conservation of mass/energy, states that there is no creation or destruction of mass/energy. The Second Law of Thermodynamics, or the law of entropy, states that all systems tend to move from order to disorder, with available energy becoming less and less.[16] Both of these laws are testable and observable in the natural world, and are consistent with a universe originating from a supernatural created beginning. They are not consistent in a universe that is supposedly increasing in complexity due to the general theory of evolution.[17]

Heredity is defined, "Biol. The tendency manifested by an organism to develop in the likeness of a progenitor, because of the transmission of genetic factors in the reproductive process."[18] Scientific evidence is in agreement with the definition of heredity. Evolution contradicts this definition for it teaches that animals evolved into more complex animals which were not like their progenitors. The Bible agrees with science for it teaches that God said an animal would reproduce "according to its kind" (Gen. 1:21, 24, 25).

INSURMOUNTABLE PROBLEMS FOR THE THEORY OF EVOLUTION

Does science confirm that the general theory of evolution is not a theory, but a fact as many adamantly profess? *It has never been proven by science that:*

1. God does not exist for such proof is outside the realm of science.

2. Matter is eternal.
3. Exploding matter could produce this enormous universe.
4. Out of disorder (explosion) arose a very orderly universe.
5. Lifeless matter could evolve into plant life.
6. Life can spontaneously generate.
7. Plants evolved into animals which have hearts, eyes, brains, etc.
8. One-celled animals eventually evolved into very complex multi-celled animals until finally man evolved.
9. Conscious man, who has a sense of moral obligation, was created by that which had no conscience and no sense of moral obligation.
10. Matter, which has no mind, created man with a mind that has the power of rational thought.
11. Non-religious matter created man with religious desires and feelings.

Let us suppose that somehow algae did produce a one-celled animal. The evolutionist still must blindly believe that this one-celled animal divided into two cells and this process went on until another animal was formed. However, for the evolutionary theory to be valid there are still some insurmountable problems to explain. There must have been more than just one one-celled animal dividing into a multi-celled animal of the same kind or the new original animal would have become extinct when it died! These newly formed original animals must have evolved within a few years of each other. They must have evolved at the same place on earth. There must have been at least one male and one female. These must have successfully mated. Their offspring must be at least one male and one female and they must have successfully mated. The same process must have occurred many times with each new animal. These animals must have evolved into more and more complex animals for evolution to be true. Who can believe it?[19]

THEISTIC EVOLUTION COMPROMISES GOD'S WORD

A serious compromise of one's belief in God's work of creation is a theory called "theistic evolution." It attempts to merge God (*theistic*) with the evolutionary theory of origins. Note the following explanations:

The theistic evolutionist holds a position somewhat between that of the absolute evolutionist and the creationist. He believes that God created the materials of our universe and then guided and superintended the process by which all life has evolved from the very simplest one-celled form on up to the sophisticated forms that we know today. Evolution was God's method of bringing about the present development, though originally the materials were created by God.[20]

Theistic evolution is a position which allows the evolution of man from an amoeba to be accepted by a Christian. It views evolution as the method by which God created man and views the Genesis account as a highly figurative portrayal of what actually happened...There are basically three objections to theistic evolution. Let us examine these as they are related to a fundamental belief in God and the Bible. (1) Man's soul cannot rationally be fitted into theistic evolution...(2) There is no real evidence to support theistic evolution...(3) To accept theistic evolution is to essentially discard the Bible.[21]

The Bible and the general theory of evolution are diametrically opposed. The only conclusion is that "a Christian cannot be a theistic evolutionist. The two are incompatible, and one who teaches evolution is teaching a false and dangerous doctrine."[22] God does not look with favor on cowardly Christians that try to appease false teachers by compromising the truth! We must not put question marks (doubts) in people's minds where God placed periods as some are doing by teaching that one may understand God's account of creation either figuratively or literally.

WHY DO MANY BELIEVE IN EVOLUTION AND NOT GOD?

Many believe in evolution and not God because they do not want to be held accountable for their thoughts, words, and actions. "So then each of us shall give account of himself to God" (Rom. 14:12). They do not want their lives controlled by a higher authority. In a letter to the editor of a large newspaper, one person stated, "...I have walked both paths, that of an unbeliever and now a believer. I can say that my 'unbelieving' lifestyle was merely an excuse for a lack of moral accountability and a ticket to live life on my terms."[23] "The late Sir Arthur Keith, noted British anthropologist, said, 'Evolution is unproved and unprovable, and the only reason we accept it is because it is the only alternative to special creation and that is unthinkable."[24] "The fool has said in his heart, 'There is no God'" (Psa. 14:1).

THE TERRIBLE CONSEQUENCES OF BELIEF IN EVOLUTION

If man believes that he is only the highest evolved animal, then when he dies that is the end of his existence for he does not have an immortal soul. He lives without hope of living in a better place after death. He lives a sad, despondent life for he does not know the answer to the question, "What is the meaning of my existence?" He does not know the loving Creator.

> If there is no real meaning or purpose in man's existence, how can a parent convince a child that the taking of drugs, or even committing suicide, is wrong? When faith in God is abandoned, the old, general, moral standards will continue to hold for a brief generation, but then will come the deluge. In America, we are beginning to reap the bitter fruits of a generation which has to an increasing degree lost faith in God. When the young are told that our entire civilization is founded on nothing morally solid they find themselves without a foundation upon which to stand, standards by which to live, and goals toward which to strive. They can really be sure of nothing. No wonder they are often angry, rebellious, violent, and destructive.[25]

God has revealed how ancient man descended into the filth of sin whenever he refused to retain God in his knowledge (Rom. 1:28-31), and walked according to his own wisdom (Eph. 4:17-19). When man does that which is "right in his own eyes," he always digresses into a wicked lifestyle for he justifies his sinful desires (Judg. 21:25). Our modern world is illustrating that same descent into wickedness as the belief in evolution becomes more widespread.

BELIEF IN GOD AS THE ETERNAL CREATOR

Belief in God elevates man for the Bible gives him the highest standard of morality. It teaches him to deny self (Matt. 16:24) by practicing self-control (Gal. 5:22, 23, 2 Pet. 1:5-7). It teaches him to love his fellow man by placing others above his own selfish interests (Matt. 22:36-40; Phil. 2:3, 4). He knows that his purpose on earth is to "Fear God and keep His commandments" (Eccl. 12:13). He serves a loving and merciful God who cares for him (Eph. 2:4; 1 Pet. 5:7) and is his help and refuge (Psa. 9:9, 10; Psa. 121). Because of the death of the Son of God, whose blood will wash away his sins in baptism, he lives with the hope of living in heaven after death (Jn. 3:16; Rev. 1:5; Acts 22:16; 1 Pet. 1:3, 4). "And God will wipe away every tear from their eyes; there shall be no more death, nor sorrow, nor crying;

and there shall be no more pain, for the former things have passed away" (Rev. 21:4).

Questions

1. What is an axiom? _a generally accepted universal truth._

2. Name two axioms. _____

   _____

3. The choices for the origin of the universe and life are eternal _____ or eternal _____.

4. Both choices must be accepted by _____.

5. Who made God? _____

   _____

6. If one does not believe in God, what does one believe is the explanation of the existence of life? _____

   _____

   _____

7. The scientific method requires that an experiment be _____ and _____.

8. Name two things that have been proven by science that agrees with the Bible. _____

   _____

9. Define theistic evolution. _____

   _____

   _____

10. Can a faithful Christian be a theistic evolutionist? Why or why not? __

    _____

    _____

Yes or No

1. Has macroevolution been proven to be true? _____

2. Has microevolution been proven to be true? _Yes_

3. Is there only one "missing link" in the evolutionary chain? _No_

4. Can science discover how the universe and life originated? _No_

5. Can science discover how God created all things? _No_

6. Does it make any difference if one believes Genesis 1 is figurative or literal? _Yes_

SCIENCE HAS NEVER PROVEN THAT:

1. _God_ does not exist.

2. _Matter_ is eternal.

3. Exploding _matter_ could produce the _universe_.

4. Out of _disorder_ came an _orderly_ universe.

5. _Lifeless_ matter could _evolve_ into _plant_ life.

6. Life can _Spontaneously_ generate.

7. Plants _evolved_ into _animals_.

8. One-celled _animals_ evolved into multi-celled _animals_.

9. Mindless matter _created_ into _man_ who has a _mind_.

10. Non-religious _matter_ could create man with _religious_ desires.

THOUGHT QUESTIONS

1. What are some of the problems with the "Big Bang Theory"?
   How can disorder create an orderly universe?

2. What are some blessings of believing in God as your Eternal Creator?
   Entering into the Kingdom
   Loving others and doing good to them.

The Triune
NATURE OF GOD

The triune nature of God is one of the most interesting, yet difficult, aspects of the one true God to understand. The concept of a triune nature of God would seem to be contradictory – how can there be one God, yet three who share the essence of that God? We must believe what the Scriptures reveal to us, no matter how difficult, or strange, it may seem.[1] Let us strive to understand this wonderful and awesome truth about our God, and stand ready to refute any false doctrine that would deny the truth about the triune nature of God.[2]

THE ONE GOD

The Jewish Scriptures declared, "Hear, O Israel: the Lord our God, the Lord is one!" (Deut. 6:4; Mk. 12:29).[3] God declared, "I am the Lord, and there is no other; there is no God besides Me" (Isa. 45:5; cf. 46:9; Deut. 4:35, 39). These truths were affirmed to Israel by God so that they would "have no other gods before Me" (Ex. 20:3). The true nature of God is monotheistic ("one God"), and not polytheistic ("many gods"). Polytheistic religions were found in the pagan religions of the Canaanites and Egyptians, along with Greek and Roman mythology around the time of Christ, to modern-day examples such as Mormonism, Hinduism, and Wicca.[4,5]

Men have created many false religions filled with multiple false idols and gods. We would do well to heed the inspired admonition, "Little children, keep yourselves from idols" (1 Jn. 5:21). An "idol" is anything, physical or mental, that replaces God as our number one priority. The apostle Paul identified covetousness (greed, love of money) as "idolatry" (Col. 3:5). Paul pleaded with idolaters in Lystra to "turn from these vain things to the living God, who made the heavens, the earth, the sea, and all things that are in them" (Acts 14:15). He commended the Thessalonians who had "turned to God from idols to serve the living and true God" (1 Thess. 1:9). We are informed that the demons even believe that there is "one God" (Jas. 2:19). A clear and unmistakable line is drawn between the one true God and the false gods of men:

> ...we know that an idol is nothing in the world, and that there is no other God but one. For even if there are so-called gods, whether in heaven or on earth (as there are many gods and many lords), yet for us there is only one God, the Father, of whom are all things, and we for Him; and one Lord Jesus Christ, through whom are all things, and through whom we live (1 Cor. 8:4-6).
> ...one God and Father of all, who is above all, and through all, and in you all (Eph. 4:6).

THE "PLURALITY" OF GOD

In lesson 2 ("The Names of God"), it is noted that the general word translated "God" in the Hebrew Scriptures is *elohim*, a plural form of *eloah*. This was a common word used in the ancient world, but it takes on greater significance when referring to the one true God. When man was created by God, both plural and singular pronouns were used: "Then God said, 'Let **Us** make man in **Our** image, according to **Our** likeness'...So God created man in **His** own image..." (Gen. 1:26, 27). In these early verses of the Bible, the plurality and singularity of God is revealed – **plural in person and singular in essence.**

Again, in the story of the tower of Babel, a plural pronoun is used by God: "Come, let **Us** go down and there confuse their language, that they may not understand one another's speech" (Gen. 11:7). At the same time, it is said that the "Lord [*Yahweh*] confused the language of all the earth" (v. 9). The Lord God is plural in person, but one in being.

This understanding of the "plurality" of God is in accord with New Testament teaching. "In the beginning was the Word, and the Word was with God, and the Word was God" (Jn. 1:1). How could the Word be God and be *with* God at the same time unless the nature of the one God entails a plurality of persons? One who searches the Scriptures will find that there are *three* persons who share the essence and nature of God (deity).[6]

Consider the following explanation of the essence and unity of God:

> When we speak of the unity of God we have in mind two things:
> 1). that there is but one infinite, eternal, self-existent Being; one

essence; 2). that this one essence is undivided and indivisible. This doctrine is taught all through the Bible...We do not affirm that one God is three Gods; we affirm that there is but one infinite Spirit Being, but within that one Spirit essence there are three personal distinctions, each of which may be, and is, called God; each capable of loving and being loved by the others; each having a distinct, but not separate, part to play in the creation of the universe, and in the creation and salvation of man.[7]

"Deity"

The term "God" refers to that which is "deity," which is defined as "divine character or nature, esp. that of the Supreme Being; divinity."[8] It is not a formal name, but a descriptive title. To say there is "one true God" speaks of one true divinity (or divine character, nature, being), and that there are no other "divinities" to compete with or to replace this one. It says nothing about the number of personalities that may share this divine essence.

A similar concept would be the term "humanity," which is defined as "the quality and condition of being human; human nature."[9] This term does not indicate how many personalities share the essence of humanity, just that, whether it is one or many, they all share the same nature of one humanity. The terms deity (God) and humanity (man) are similar concepts indicating nature and essence. Of course, deity is the Creator and humanity is the created. The essence of deity is greater and higher than that of humanity (Isa. 40:28; 55:8-9).

"Godhead"

The term "Godhead" is a translation of the Greek word theiotes in Romans 1:20, theotes in Colossians 2:9, and theios in Acts 17:29. All three words have reference to the divine nature and essence of Deity (Godhood):

In the first (Rom. i. 20) St. Paul is declaring how much of God may be known from the revelation of Himself which He has made in nature, from those vestiges of Himself which men may everywhere trace in the world around them. Yet it is not the personal God whom any man may learn to know by these aids; He can be known only by the revelation of Himself in his Son.[10]

But in the second passage (Col. ii. 9) St. Paul is declaring that in the Son there dwells all the fullness of absolute Godhead; they were no mere rays of divine glory which gilded Him, lighting up his person for a season and with a splendour not his own; but He was, and is, absolute and perfect God; and the Apostle uses *theotes* to express the essential and personal Godhead of the Son.[11]

In Acts 17:29 it is used as a noun with the definite article, to denote "the Godhead," the Deity (i.e. the one true God).[12]

The term "Godhead" itself does not reveal the triune nature of God. It only speaks to the glorious, divine nature that is God. Nevertheless, the three distinct persons who share the essence of this "Godhead" are revealed in the New Testament as the *Father, Son, and Holy Spirit*. They are not three distinct Gods, nor are they partitions of one divine Person. The truth about the unity, relationship, and interaction of the "one God in three persons" is revealed in the Scriptures for man to understand and believe.

THREE THAT ARE ONE: THE FATHER, SON, AND HOLY SPIRIT

The New Testament reveals that three share the essence and nature of God: *the Father, Son, and Holy Spirit*. While equal in essence, they each have their particular role and work.[13] This is why it can be said that the Son is equal with God (Jn. 5:18 – *essence*), and, at the same time, that the Father is greater than the Son (Jn. 14:28 – *role of subjection*).

GOD THE FATHER

God the Father (Phil. 2:11) is described in various ways:

Father of our Lord Jesus Christ (Col. 1:3)
Father of mercies (2 Cor. 1:3)
Father of spirits (Heb. 12:9)
Father of lights (Jas. 1:17)
Who is in heaven (Matt. 6:9)
The throne of the Father (Rev. 3:21)

The Father is the reconciler of man to God by sending his Son (Col. 1:19-22; 2 Cor. 5:17-21; Jn. 3:16; 6:57). Those who are adopted into his family can address him as "Abba, Father" (Gal. 4:6). We are to address our prayers to the Father (Matt. 6:9), and strive to be perfect as he is (Matt. 5:48).

GOD THE SON

God the Son is divine, equal to the Father (Jn. 1:1; 5:18). Previously, he was the Word (Jn. 1:1), and was born of Mary in order to partake in flesh and blood that he might give his life for mankind (Matt. 1:23; Heb. 2:14; Phil. 2:5-8). He became our redeemer by means of death in order to offer up his own blood for all the faithful (Heb. 9:11-15).

The Son is the promised Messiah [Christ] (Matt. 16:16). He is presently head over the church (Eph. 1:22-23), king over his kingdom (Acts 2:30; Col. 1:13), High Priest (Heb. 8:1), and "Mediator between God and men" (1 Tim. 2:5). He will return someday and hand the kingdom back to the Father (1 Cor. 15:23-26). He will raise the dead, judge all mankind, and take his people to heaven for eternity (Jn. 5:28-29; 2 Cor. 5:10; 1 Thess. 4:17).

GOD THE HOLY SPIRIT

God the Holy Spirit is seen in the beginning (Gen. 1:2), and in Old Testament times (1 Sam. 11:6). The Spirit revealed God's word to man in the Old Testament (Zech. 7:12; 2 Pet. 1:21) and, as the Comforter, revealed the New Testament (Jn. 14:26; 16:13; 1 Cor. 2:9-13; Eph. 3:3-5). The Holy Spirit also provided the gifts of the Spirit that guided men in the first century, beginning on the day of Pentecost (Acts 2:16-21, 33; 1 Cor. 12:7-11). We are now "sealed with the Holy Spirit of promise, who is the guarantee of our inheritance until the redemption of the purchased possession" (Eph. 1:13-14).

THE FATHER, SON, AND HOLY SPIRIT WORKING TOGETHER

The Father, Son, and Holy Spirit all work together for the redemption of sinful man. Jesus promised the apostles before his death: "But when the Helper comes, whom I shall send to you from the Father, the Spirit of truth who proceeds from the Father, He will testify of Me" (Jn. 15:26). The Father sent the Son, who then sent the Holy Spirit, to reveal the gospel message to man through the apostles and prophets.

Jesus commanded the apostles to "Go therefore and make disciples of all the nations, baptizing them in the name of the Father and of the Son and of the Holy Spirit" (Matt. 28:19). Here each one is placed upon an equal level of authority in the salvation of man under one "name." This could not be possible unless all three shared the same essence and nature of deity.[14] The complete work of salvation accomplished for man by the triune God is noted by Peter when he wrote about Christians being "elect according to the foreknowledge of God the Father, in sanctification of the Spirit, for obedience and sprinkling of the blood of Jesus Christ" (1 Pet. 1:2).

The unity of the Father, Son, and Holy Spirit while providing the variety of spiritual gifts in the church of the first century is clearly set forth: "Now there are diversities of gifts, but the same Spirit. There are differences of ministries, but the same Lord. And there are diversities of activities, but it is the same God who works all in all" (1 Cor. 12:4-6).

All who have obeyed the gospel enjoy the fellowship of the triune God: "Now He who establishes us with you in Christ and has anointed us is God, who also has sealed us and given us the Spirit in our hearts as a deposit" (2 Cor. 1:21-22). There is complete unity of will, purpose, and action of the Father, Son, and Holy Spirit for our spiritual and eternal benefit.[15]

FALSE DOCTRINES DENYING THE TRIUNE GOD
False doctrines of man have arisen that deny the truth about the triune nature of the one God. These doctrines contradict the truth and will destroy our faith. While some "twist" the scriptures concerning the nature of God (2 Pet. 3:16), let us test all things and hold fast to that which is good (1 Thess. 5:21).

POLYTHEISM
Some believe that the triune nature of God is equal to polytheism (the belief in many gods). As stated earlier, the Bible teaches that there is one God, not many (Deut. 6:4; Isa. 45:5). Polytheism is a human doctrine that creates a realm where separate gods of different natures and essences exist. Modern day examples include Mormonism.[16] The demons believe that there is one God, and so should we (Jas. 2:19)! The false gods of polytheistic religions are to be rejected. God says to them, "Indeed you are nothing, and your work is nothing; he who chooses you is an abomination" (Isa. 41:24).

JESUS IS A CREATED BEING
Some believe that Jesus was a created being. A Jehovah's Witness publication states the following:

> ...the Bible plainly states that in his prehuman existence, Jesus was a created spirit being, just as angels were spirit beings created by God. Neither the angels nor Jesus had existed before their creation...Jehovah God alone is Almighty. He created the prehuman

Jesus directly. Thus, Jesus had a beginning and could never be coequal with God in power or eternity.[17]

Furthermore, the Jehovah's Witnesses have mistranslated John 1:1 in their New World Translation making it to say that the Word was "a god." Such is not the case, for the Son is called in prophecy "Mighty God" and "Everlasting Father" (Isa. 9:6). Jesus is addressed as the eternal Jehovah (*Yahweh*) (Heb. 1:10-12) who was in the form of God and equal with God (Phil. 2:6). Jesus referred to himself as the "I AM" (Jn. 8:58; Ex. 3:14).

Jesus is not a created being, for the Scriptures affirm that *all things* were created by him and for him, that he might have the preeminence as the Creator (Col. 1:15-18; Jn. 1:3). "Preeminent position" is the meaning of the phrase "firstborn over all creation" (Col. 1:15). Jesus has this pre-eminent position of supremacy and honor due to the fact that he is the Creator of all creation.[18] These truths also help us understand what Jesus meant when he described himself as the "Beginning of the creation of God" (Rev. 3:14). "This does not mean he is the first person or thing created by God, but that he is the source or originating cause (*arche*); he is the active agent of God by whom all things were created."[19]

HOLY SPIRIT IS NOT A PERSON OR GOD
Some deny that the Holy Spirit is a person, or God. Again, a Jehovah's Witness publication states:

> The Bible's use of "holy spirit" indicates that it is a controlled force that Jehovah God uses to accomplish a variety of his purposes. To a certain extent, it can be likened to electricity, a force that can be adapted to perform a great variety of operations…No, the holy spirit is not a person and it is not part of a Trinity. The holy spirit is God's active force that he uses to accomplish his will. It is not equal to God but is always at his disposition and subordinate to him.[20]

The Bible speaks of the Holy Spirit in personal terms (Jn. 16:13 "He, the Spirit of truth"). He also possesses personality because he speaks (1 Tim. 4:1; Acts 8:29; 10:19; 13:2), teaches/guides (Jn. 14:26; 16:13), has a will (1 Cor. 12:11), can be grieved (Eph. 4:30), insulted (Heb. 10:29), lied to (Acts 5:3), and resisted (Acts 7:51). The term "God" and "Holy Spirit" are used interchangeably (Acts 5:3, 4). The Spirit searches and knows the mind of God (1 Cor. 2:10-11). A force "likened to electricity" cannot search and know the infinite mind of God. Such is the foolishness of the doctrines of men.

"ONENESS" PENTECOSTALISM

The doctrine of "Oneness" is that the Godhead consists of but one Personality who manifests Himself in various functions, identified as Father, Son, and Holy Ghost. There are not three Personalities, it is asserted; the Father, Son, and Holy Spirit are not distinct.[21]

This idea that only one Personality exists as the Father, Son, and Holy Spirit breeds incredible confusion in understanding the Scriptures. How can the baptism of Jesus make any sense with the Son being baptized, the Father speaking from heaven, and the Holy Spirit descending if all this was accomplished by *one person* (Matt. 3:16-17; Lk. 3:21-22)? It makes nonsense of Jesus' words about the Father knowing what the Son does not know (Mk. 13:32). If the Father and the Son are actually one divine Person, how can that one person know and not know the same thing at the same time? It makes nonsense of other statements of Jesus (Lk. 23:46; Jn. 8:16-18; 14:16). Was Stephen confused when he saw the vision of heaven and Jesus at the right hand of God (Acts 7:55)? The ones who are confused are those deceived by these false doctrines of men.

GLORIFYING THE ONE TRUE GOD

We must trust God by obeying and living the truth that he has revealed to us. We must uphold the truth about the unity of the one God and the three persons within that divine relationship – the Father, Son, and Holy Spirit. Let us not be ashamed of this truth, but speak it boldly in a world that needs to know about our God and Creator. "The grace of the Lord Jesus Christ, and the love of God, and the communion of the Holy Spirit be with you all. Amen" (2 Cor. 13:14).

❧ QUESTIONS ❧

1. How many true Gods are revealed in the Bible? _____

2. List some polytheistic religions, both ancient and modern. _____

_____

3. What words in Genesis 1:26 indicate the "plurality" of God? _____

_____

_____

4. What is the definition of "deity"? _____

_____

_____

5. How are the concepts of deity and humanity similar? _____

_____

_____

6. List the three passages where the term "Godhead" is found. _____

_____

_____

7. Who are the three distinct persons who share the essence of God? _____

_____

8. List some unique aspects of:

a. God the Father _____

_____

_____

b. God the Son _____

_____

_____

c. God the Holy Spirit _____

_____

_____

9. List four passages that speak of the Father, Son, and Holy Spirit working together. _____

_____

10. Why is polytheism a false doctrine? _____

_____

11. Cite a Bible passage that proves that Jesus could not be a created being. _____

12. What are some of the personality traits of the Holy Spirit? _____

_____

_____

13. How can we know that the Father, Son, and Holy Spirit do not all exist as one person? _____

_____

_____

FILL IN THE BLANK AND GIVE THE SCRIPTURE

1. "Hear, O Israel: the Lord our _____, the Lord is _____!"
   (_____)

2. "Come, let _____ go down and there confuse their language…"
   (_____)

3. "In the beginning was the _____, and the Word was _____ God, and the Word was _____." (_____)

TRUE OR FALSE

God is:
1. ____ three distinct Gods
2. ____ three partitions of one Person
3. ____ three distinct persons sharing one essence
4. ____ many gods with different natures

THOUGHT QUESTIONS

1. If a Jehovah's Witness told you that you believe in "three Gods," how should you respond?

2. Explain why Jesus' statement, "My Father is greater than I" (Jn. 14:28) *does not contradict* the fact that the Son and the Father are equal as God [deity] (Phil. 2:6; Jn. 5:18

THE "ALL" POWER, KNOWLEDGE, AND PRESENCE OF GOD

The Bible reveals that the one true God is a powerful, knowledgeable, and ever-present being. But God is not just one powerful, knowledgeable, and ever-present being among many other such beings. Our God is all-powerful, all-knowing, and all-present greater and above anyone in heaven and on earth. These attributes are often called the *omnipotence, omniscience,* and *omnipresence* of God. The prefix "omni-" is "a combining form meaning 'all,' used in the formation of compound words: *omnifarious; omnipotence; omniscient.*"[1] These terms perfectly capture the glory and greatness that is the God of heaven and earth. This lesson will explore these attributes more closely.

THE OMNIPOTENCE OF GOD

The "omnipotence" of God refers to the fact that God is all-powerful in every possible way. Man imagines himself as very powerful. He can construct large machines that can change landscapes, computers that can quickly perform complicated tasks, and build weapons that could destroy millions of lives. Yet these do not even begin to compare to the awesome power of God. We see great forces of nature such as hurricanes and earthquakes that cause many to fear for their lives. Yet, again, these only give us a small glimpse into the incredible power of God.

The names of God speak of his power. *El,* and its plural form, *Elohim,* refer to the power and preeminence of God.[2] God referred to himself as *El Shaddai,* the Almighty God (Gen. 17:1). When we speak of God, we need to always be reminded of his great might. As the Lord himself asked, "Is anything too hard for the Lord?" (Gen. 18:14; Jer. 32:17, 27; Num. 11:23).

King Nebuchadnezzar, one of the most powerful kings in history, had to admit that the true God of heaven "does according to His will in the army of heaven and among the inhabitants of the earth. No one can restrain His hand or say to Him, 'What have You done?'" (Dan. 4:35). Those who consider themselves as mighty and powerful among men today would do well to remember what Nebuchadnezzar learned, and to heed the voice that said, "Alleluia! For the Lord God Omnipotent reigns!" (Rev. 19:6).

The awesome power of God has been demonstrated in the following ways:

CREATION

The apostle Paul declared that "since the creation of the world His invisible attributes are clearly seen, being understood by the things that are made, even His eternal power and Godhead..." (Rom. 1:20). As we increase our knowledge of this material universe, we should be ever more impressed with the power of the one true God who created it and sustains it (Jer. 32:17)

By simply the power of his word, God created all things from nothing (Heb. 11:3). As the Psalmist declares, "By the word of the Lord the heavens were made, and all the host of them by the breath of His mouth...Let all the earth fear the Lord; let all the inhabitants of the world stand in awe of Him. For He spoke, and it was done; He commanded, and it stood fast" (Psa. 33:6, 8-9).

Job spoke concerning God's power as he observed the wonder of the created world:

> He stretches out the north over empty space; He hangs the earth on nothing. He binds up the water in His thick clouds, yet the clouds are not broken under it. He covers the face of His throne, and spreads His cloud over it. He drew a circular horizon on the face of the waters, at the boundary of light and darkness. The pillars of heaven tremble, and are astonished at His reproof. He stirs up the sea with His power, and by His understanding He breaks up the storm. By His Spirit He adorned the heavens; His hand pierced the fleeing serpent. Indeed these are the mere edges of His ways, and how small a whisper we hear of Him! But the thunder of His power who can understand? (Job 26:7-14).

WORKS

"The works of the Lord are great, studied by all who have pleasure in them...He has declared to His people the power of His works, in giving them the heritage of the nations" (Psa. 111:2, 6). Mankind is invited to "come and see the works of God; He is awesome in His doing toward the sons of men" (Psa. 66:5). We can even marvel at how God formed each one of us: "For You have formed my inward parts; You have covered me in my mother's womb. I will praise You, for I am fearfully and wonderfully made; marvelous are Your works, and that my soul knows very well" (Psa. 139:13-14).

God does not, and will not, grow tired: "The everlasting God, the Lord, the Creator of the ends of the earth, neither faints nor is weary" (Isa. 40:28). The power of God is only limited by his will: "Whatever the Lord pleases He does, in heaven and in earth, in the seas and in all the deep places" (Psa. 135:6). Therefore, we can be so thankful that "the works of His hands are verity and justice; all His precepts are sure. They stand fast forever and ever, and are done in truth and uprightness" (Psa. 111:7-8).[3]

SALVATION

Israel of old was delivered from Egyptian bondage by God's "mighty hand" and "out-stretched arm" (Deut. 5:15), and mankind today is delivered from the bondage of sin by the gospel of Christ which is the "power of God to salvation for everyone who believes" (Rom. 1:16). The truth of God may seem like foolishness to some, but to those who are being saved it is the "power of God" (1 Cor. 1:18). Our faith should "not be in the wisdom of men but in the power of God" (1 Cor. 2:5), and the word of God continues to be "living and powerful" for all who live by it (Heb. 4:12).

The power of God was at work in the raising of Jesus from the dead and placing him above all things (Eph. 1:19-23). For man this power is exhibited in raising him up from the death of sin to be made alive in Christ (2:1-6). Nothing but the wisdom and power of God could have accomplished such a powerful salvation for sinners who were "without strength" (Rom. 5:6).

THE OMNISCIENCE OF GOD

The "omniscience" of God refers to God's all-encompassing knowledge of all things. It is difficult for man's finite mind to even begin to comprehend a divine mind that is all-knowing. Man may gather great print and digital libraries filled with all the available knowledge of human history and exploration, but this could only be as a tiny speck of the deep knowledge of the Creator. His "knowing" is not only all-encompassing, but fully accurate in every way. God knows the truth about everything, everywhere, at every time. Truly, there is "no searching of His understanding" (Isa. 40:28)

The Psalmist spoke with great wonder about the omniscience of God:

> O Lord, You have searched me and known me. You know my sitting down and my rising up; You understand my thought afar off. You comprehend my path and my lying down, and are acquainted with all my ways. For there is not a word on my tongue, but behold, O Lord, You know it altogether. You have hedged me behind and before, and laid Your hand upon me. Such knowledge is too wonderful to me; it is high, I cannot attain it" (Psa. 139:1-6).

The knowledge of God encompasses the totality of the past, present, and future. "He stands in a sense above time, so that his consciousness embraces the whole of time in a single act of knowing. His knowledge of the past and the future is as real and infallible as his knowledge of the present."[4] An identifying mark of deity is the ability to "know the former things, what they were...and know the latter end of them; or declare... things to come...the things that are to come hereafter" (Isa. 41:22, 23). The false gods (idols) of men cannot know such things, for they are "nothing" (v. 24). Only the true God in heaven knows all things perfectly.

THE PAST

God knows all past history perfectly and was able to guide men of old to write the history in the Scriptures with perfect accuracy (2 Pet. 1:21). As the scriptures further state, "Known to God from eternity are all His works" (Acts 15:18).

THE PRESENT

God knows all things that happen at every present moment. Solomon declared, "The eyes of the Lord are in every place, keeping watch on the evil and the good" (Prov. 15:3; cf. Job 34:21; Zech. 4:10; Psa. 33:13-14). In this passage we see the convergence of the omnipotence, omniscience, and omnipresence of God. God is *all-present* because he is *all-powerful* and is, therefore, *all-knowing*. Everything and everyone is exposed and open before the all-seeing eye of God (Heb. 4:13).

THE FUTURE

God is able to know things that have not yet happened. The inspired prophecies of Scriptures affirm this fact. How could Isaiah prophesy by name about a future king of Persia, Cyrus, nearly 200 years before he was born (Isa. 44:28-45:3)? How could Daniel inform Nebuchadnezzar about the kingdoms to follow his without God who "reveals secrets" and makes known "what will be in the latter days" (Dan. 2:28)? And we have not even mentioned the multiple prophecies of Jesus spoken centuries before he was born. One of the marks of deity is the ability to declare "the end from the beginning, and from ancient times things that are not yet done" (Isa. 46:10; 48:3-7). God is not limited by time nor by a finite mind. The depth of God's mind transcends the limits of time and space.

The ability of God to know all things past, present, and future makes him a perfect and just judge. "For God will bring every work into judgment, including every secret thing, whether it be good or whether it is evil" (Eccl. 12:14). When the Lord comes he will "bring to light the hidden things of darkness and reveal the counsels of the hearts" (1 Cor. 4:5; 1 Jn. 3:20). God knows the sins of the sinner, and will not forget the labor of the righteous (Heb. 6:10; 1 Cor. 15:58). Truly, "great is our Lord, and mighty in power; His understanding is infinite. The Lord lifts up the humble; He casts the wicked down to the ground" (Psa. 147:5-6).

THE OMNIPRESENCE OF GOD

The "omnipresence" refers to the ever-present nature of God. God's presence is not limited by space for "he is universally present to all of space at all time."[5] There is no place that we can go to escape the presence of God. The Psalmist writes:

> Where can I go from Your Spirit? Or where can I flee from Your presence? If I ascend into heaven, You are there; if I make my bed in hell, behold, You are there. If I take the wings of the morning, and dwell in the uttermost parts of the sea, even there Your hand shall lead me, and Your right hand shall hold me. If I say, "Surely the darkness shall fall on me," even the night shall be light about me; indeed, the darkness shall not hide from You, but the night shines as the day; the darkness and the light are both alike to You (Psa. 139:7-12).

God describes himself as omnipresent: "'Am I a God near at hand?' says the Lord, 'And not a God afar off? Can anyone hide himself in secret places, so I shall not see him?' says the Lord; 'Do I not fill heaven and earth?' says the Lord" (Jer. 23:23-24; 1 Kgs. 8:27). We must be careful, though, to distinguish between the *presence* of God and the *person* of God:

> God is found in all places by the instrumentality of His creation, laws, works, agents, appointments, manifestations, etc., while His person is in heaven. *Omnipresence does not mean that God's person is everywhere*, but rather His presence is everywhere by way of the preceding avenues mentioned. The Bible does not teach the *omniperson* of God, but rather it teaches the *omnipresence* of God. To teach that the person of God is everywhere is to teach a form of pantheism, the belief that the universe is God and God is the universe. Though Jehovah is both transcendant (separate from and beyond the material universe) and immanent (with us), He is not *omniperson*.[6]

"Theophanies," or appearances of God in physical time and space, are described in the Bible (e.g. Gen. 18:1; Ex. 24:9-11). "God's omnipresence does not prevent Him from manifesting Himself in a localized place...He has, at various times, entered space at specific points and become present in it for a specific purpose."[7] Such appearances did not limit God's omnipresence in any way. His presence continually fills heaven and earth at all times.

The Bible teaches the possibility of being cast from God's "presence." Cain "went out from the presence of the Lord" (Gen. 4:16). The kingdom of Judah was sent away from God's presence into Babylonian captivity (2 Kgs. 24:3, 20). The idea here is the "rejection of God, separated from Him, losing God's protection and standing defenseless against their enemies."[8] Eternal punishment in hell will be "everlasting destruction from the presence of the Lord and from the glory of His power" (2 Thess. 1:9). God has prepared hell as a place of divine justice upon evil and wickedness that will be absent God's comfort, fellowship and blessings.

FALSE CONCEPTS

One false concept concerning these attributes of God is that if God is all-powerful and all-loving, then evil should not exist. This argument (called "the problem of evil") is used to deny the existence of the God of the Bible. It is argued that since evil exists in the world, then a God does not exist that is all-powerful (or he *could* have created a world without evil) or all-loving (or he *would* destroy evil). This argument fails to consider two important factors: man's *freedom of choice* and the *longsuffering* of God.

Man was created with volition, or the ability to choose his ow[n]
in this world is the result of man choosing to do evil (Rom. 3:10
forbade evil to exist, then man would not have the ability to ᴄɦoose his
own path, but be forced to choose only righteousness. God certainly has
the power to destroy evil. God also loves all men, sending his Son into
the world to be a sin-sacrifice destroying the power of Satan and giving
man the hope of eternal salvation (Jn. 3:16; Heb. 2:14). He did not, and
has not, immediately destroyed Satan and evil, not because he is slow,
powerless, or loveless, but "is longsuffering toward us, not willing that any
should perish but that all should come to repentance" (2 Pet. 3:9). Every
atheist should be thankful that God is loving and longsuffering, giving
them ample opportunity to repent!

Another false concept is that God cannot know the future since it has
not happened in reality yet, and such knowledge would contradict man's
freedom of choice. In other words, it is impossible to know what has not
yet happened, and if God does know it, then our actions have been pre-
determined, not freely chosen. This reasoning wrongly places God's *foreknowledge* against man's *free choice*. Additionally, this argument

> places a limitation on the power and sovereignty of God insofar
> as it is stated that God *cannot* know truly free choices ahead of
> time, or that he can know them only if he predetermines them.
> …the only view that preserves both the integrity of God's fore-
> knowledge and the integrity of human free will is the view that
> God foreknows future contingent choices simply because he is the
> transcendent God who stands above time and knows all things in
> an eternal now.[9]

God foreknew and prophesied the events surrounding the death of Jesus (Acts 2:23; 4:27-28), but those involved (Judas, Pilate, Jewish leaders,
etc.) were responsible for their own actions. Those responsible for putting
Jesus to death chose to be greedy, cowardly, and envious, and needed to
repent. God is no respecter of persons (Acts 10:34), and has not predeter-
mined anyone's eternal destiny regardless of his own choices and actions.

LESSONS TO REMEMBER

First, great *comfort* is provided to the faithful Christian in knowing that
God is all powerful, all-knowing, and all-present. We do not have to be
like the prophets of Baal, acting like fools in trying to wake up a false god
to take notice and help them (1 Kgs. 18:26-29). The true God of heaven
is never asleep, out to lunch, or away on a journey. He is ever present,

knows everything we think and need, and is sufficiently powerful to help us. Jesus promised, "For where two or three are gathered together in My name, I am there in the midst of them" (Matt. 18:20).

Second, we should *fear* (reverence, respect) God who has unlimited power, who knows all things, and from whom we cannot hide (Matt. 10:28). Too many in today's world give no thought to the Creator and Sustainer of their lives, "for in Him we live and move and have our being" (Acts 17:28). Our purpose in life is to "fear God and keep His commandments" (Eccl. 12:13). When the final day of judgment comes, God will not overlook anyone. The labor of the righteous will be rewarded and the wickedness of men will receive just punishment (2 Thess. 1:5-10). We ignore God to our own eternal peril!

Third, living a *hypocritical life* is utterly foolish and destructive. We may fool those around us who cannot know our secret sins and evil thoughts, but God does see and God does know. Nothing can be hidden from his sight nor will it escape his mind. Moses wrote, "You have set our iniquities before You, our secret sins in the light of Your countenance" (Psa. 90:8). David prayed that the Lord would cleanse him from "secret faults" (Psa. 19:12). Every sinner must realize that God sees and knows his every way, and will bring him into judgment. You cannot hide or run away from God (ask Adam and Eve, then Jonah!). Developing a sense of the presence of God will help us flee from sin.

Fourth, we are blessed by the *providential care* of God who sees and knows our every step, temptation, sorrow, and need. The word of his power directs our paths and lifts up our hearts. Knowing he is ever-present keeps us strong in times of trial, for we are never alone (Heb. 13:5-6). If God numbers the hairs of our heads, can we not be fully assured that he cares for each one of us (Matt. 10:30; 1 Pet. 5:7)?

OUR UNLIMITED CREATOR

Because God is the uncreated Creator, he is not bound by the limitations of created being. He exists in a totally different way. He is unlimited in his very existence; it is his very nature to exist, and he cannot not exist. He is also unlimited with regard to space and time; he exists outside their limitations. His knowledge is likewise unlimited, as is his power. Such is the nature of the one who is the Maker of heaven and earth.[10]

Let us rejoice in our all-powerful, all-knowing, and all-present God. May the joy of this knowledge increase our faith and motivate us to greater service and worship. "Oh, the depth of the riches both of the wisdom and knowledge of God! How unsearchable are His judgments and His ways past finding out!" (Rom. 11:33).

QUESTIONS

1. What is the meaning of the "omnipotence" of God? _____
_____

2. What Hebrew names of God speak of his power? _____
_____

3. How did God demonstrate his power in creation? _____
_____
_____

4. How did God demonstrate his power in providing salvation? _____
_____

5. What is the meaning of the "omniscience" of God? _____
_____

6. How do we know that God is able to know the future? _____
_____

7. What is the meaning of the "omnipresence" of God? _____
_____

8. Where is man able to escape the presence of God? _____
_____

9. What does it mean to be cast from God's "presence"? _____
_____
_____

10. If God has the power to destroy all evil, why does he not do it immediately? _____
_____
_____

11. How is it possible for God to know the future and *not* predetermine our actions? _____

    _____

    _____

12. List four lessons we should remember in view of God's power/knowledge/presence?

    a. _____

    _____

    b. _____

    _____

    c. _____

    _____

    d. _____

    _____

FILL IN THE BLANK AND GIVE THE SCRIPTURE

1. "Is anything too _____ for the Lord?" (_____)

2. "Great is our Lord, and mighty in _____; His understanding is _____" (_____)

3. "Can anyone _____ himself in secret places, so I shall not _____ him?" (_____)

4. "For where _____ or _____ are gathered together in My name, I am _____ in the midst of them" (_____)

5. "Oh, the _____ of the riches both of the _____ and _____ of God! How _____ are His judgments and His ways _____ finding out!" (_____)

GIVE THE VERSES

Give the verses in Psalm 139 that describe God's:
1. Omniscience _____
2. Omnipresence _____
3. Omnipotence _____

THOUGHT QUESTIONS

1. How do God's power, knowledge, and presence make him a perfect and just judge?

2. How should daily meditation on these "all" attributes of God have a practical effect on our lives?

GOD IS
SPIRIT AND IS HOLY

GOD IS SPIRIT

Jesus revealed God's nature to a Samaritan woman when he said, "God is Spirit, and those who worship Him must worship in spirit and truth" (Jn. 4:24). "These words mean that God is a non-material personal being, self-conscious and self-determining."[1] Since "God is Spirit," he "does not have flesh and bones" (Lk. 24:39). His nature is incorruptible! He is in heaven (Matt. 6:9) where there is nothing that is corruptible (1 Pet. 1:4).

MORMONISM TEACHES THAT GOD IS FLESH AND BONE

"*Doctrine and Covenants*, one of the standard works of the Mormon faith, states in Section 130, verse 22: 'God the Father has a body of flesh and bone as tangible as man's.'"[2]

We quote a sermon given by Joseph Smith, Jr. two months before he was killed in Carthage, Illinois, in 1844. This sermon was heard by over 18,000 people. It was taken down by five Mormon scribes and published in the official Mormon publication *Times and Seasons*, volume 5, page 613.

It is also found in the LDS encyclopedic work *Mormon Doctrine* by Bruce R. McConkie, page 321.

God was once as we are now, an exalted man, and sits enthroned in yonder heavens. I say if you were to see him today you would see him like a man in form like yourselves and all the person and image of man. I am going to tell you how God came to be God. We have imagined that God was God from all eternity. I will refute that idea and take away the veil. God was once a man like us and dwelt on an earth, the same as Jesus Christ did, and you have got to learn to be gods yourselves the same as all gods before you. Namely by going from one small degree to another, from a small capacity to a greater one.[3]

This unscriptural doctrine may be concisely stated: "As man is, God once was, and as God is, man may become."[4]

GOD WAS NEVER FLESH AND BONE

The heavenly Father was never a man who evolved into God! "For I am God, and not man" (Hos. 11:9). Balaam said, "God is not a man, that He should lie" (Num. 23:19). He has always been a Divine being (Psa. 90:2). To teach that God was once flesh and bone is blasphemy!

When "God created man in His own image" (Gen. 1:26-27), it was not man's physical body that was made in his image. It was man's spiritual, intellectual, and emotional nature that was made in his image.

WE WILL BE RAISED WITH A SPIRITUAL BODY

Because our "flesh and blood" bodies are corruptible and mortal, they "cannot inherit the kingdom of God; nor does corruption inherit incorruption" (1 Cor. 15:50). We will be resurrected with glorious, spiritual, incorruptible, and immortal bodies (vv. 42-44, 51-54). Such bodies are suitable for "an inheritance incorruptible and undefiled and does not fade away, reserved in heaven for you" (1 Pet. 1:4).

ANTHROPOMORPHISM

Since God is Spirit, "No one has seen God at any time" (Jn. 1:18). Man is unable to see a spirit. However the Bible states: "...they saw the God of Israel" (Ex. 24:10). God said to Moses, "Then I will take away My hand and you shall see My back; but My face shall not be seen" (Ex. 33:23). These passages do not contradict each other.

Anthropomorphism is defined, "The ascription of human attributes, feelings, conduct, or characteristics to God or any spiritual being, or to the powers of nature, etc."[5] "Anthropos has reference to man; and morphis has reference to form. As applied to the discussion of God, this means that in representing God to man, God is often described in language that describes man."[6] Human body parts, such as, hands, feet, arms, eyes, ears, etc. are figuratively ascribed to God to help us understand how he acts and feels (Ex. 6:6; Isa. 59:1-2; 1 Pet. 3:12). When we speak of the "eye of the hurricane," we are using anthropomorphism.

IDOLATRY IS IRRATIONAL AND CONDEMNED

Since God is Spirit, it is impossible for a material image to look like him. "Since we do not know what pure spirit looks like, we cannot have a mental image of God... It is unnecessary for us to form a mental picture of God. If it had been necessary God would have made it possible for us to do so."[7] Any material image, that is made to represent God, is degrading to him for it is corruptible, but he is incorruptible. "Professing to be wise, they become fools, and changed the glory of the incorruptible God into an image made like corruptible man – and birds and four-footed beasts and creeping things" (Rom. 1:22-23). "Therefore, since we are the offspring of God, we ought not to think that the Divine Nature is like gold or silver or stone, something shaped by art and man's devising" (Acts 17:29). The worship of idols is condemned in both the Old and New Testaments (Ex. 20:1-6; Deut. 4:15-19; 1 Cor. 6:9-10).

GOD DOES NOT GROW OLD

Since God is Spirit, he is not subject to sickness, decay, or death. The passing of time does not diminish his strength, hearing, eyesight, memory, etc. It is wonderful to know that he is never asleep, or too tired or sick to hear our prayers, or too weak "to help us in time of need" (Heb. 4:16). He will not forget us (2 Tim. 2:19).

OMNIPRESENT

Since God is Spirit and not matter, he is not confined to one place like man. A human body can only be in one place at one time. We are sometimes frustrated because we cannot be in more than one place at one time.

God is omnipresent, which means "the quality of being everywhere present at the same time."[8] Solomon acknowledged this truth when he asked, "But will God indeed dwell on earth? Behold, heaven and the heavens of heavens cannot contain You. How much less this temple which I have built!" (1 Kgs. 8:27). How can he be everywhere present? "It is beyond our grasp. God has not revealed to us the how of it, but He has revealed the fact of it."[9]

Since God's presence is everywhere, we cannot hide from him (Jer. 23:23-24; Psa. 139:1-12). He sees everything we do. "The eyes of the Lord are in every place, keeping watch on the evil and the good" (Prov. 15:3). We can worship him anywhere we live (Jn. 4:20-24). It is very comforting to know, "The Lord is at hand" (Phil. 4:4-7). "He is not far from each one of us" (Acts 17:27). The righteous are assured that "the eyes of the Lord are on the righteous and His ears are open to their prayers" (1 Pet. 3:12).

The Bible sometimes makes reference to God being in a specific location (Gen. 11:5; 18:20-21; Matt. 6:9). Do these passages contradict the passages that teach that he is everywhere? No! One must distinguish the *presence* of God and the *person* of God.[10]

GOD IS HOLY

One seraphim said to another seraphim, "Holy, holy, holy is the Lord of hosts; the whole earth is full of His glory!" (Isa. 6:3). In heaven, "four living creatures" say, "Holy, holy, holy, Lord God Almighty, who was and is and is to come!" (Rev. 4:8). This is the only attribute of God that is repeated three times in succession. This repetition gives intense emphasis to the infinite holiness of the Creator. A great difference, between "the living and true God" (1 Thess. 1:9) and the gods of other religions is that God is infinitely holy. "Who is like You, O Lord, among the gods? Who is like You, glorious in holiness...?" (Ex. 15:11). Hannah said in her prayer, "There is none holy like the Lord" (1 Sam. 2:2).

DEFINITION OF HOLY

"**Holiness, Holy,** usually translate words derived from a Heb. root *qa-dash* and Greek *hag-*. The basic meaning of *qadash* is *separateness, withdrawal*. It is first applied to God, and is early associated with purity and righteousness."[11, 12]

According to W. E. Vine, the Greek word *hagiamos*, which is translated, "holiness" "signifies (a) separation to God, 1 Cor. 1:30; 2 Thess. 2:13; 1 Pet. 1:2; (b) the resultant state, the conduct befitting those so separated, 1 Thess. 4:3, 4, 7...in Scripture in its moral and spiritual significance, separated from sin and therefore consecrated to God, sacred."[13] Something is made holy by separating it from common use to be used in the service of God.

TWO DISTINCT SENSES OF GOD'S HOLINESS

As applied to God the notion of holiness is used in the OT in two distinct senses: (1) First in the more general sense of separation from all that is human and earthly. It thus denotes the absoluteness, majesty, and awfulness of the Creator in His distinction from the creature... (2) But, in the next place, holiness of character in the distinct ethical sense is ascribed to God. The injunction, "Be ye holy; for I am holy" (Lev. 11:44; 19:2), plainly implies an ethical conception.[14]

"While ontological holiness signifies God's separateness from creatures as such, ethical holiness refers to his separateness from *sin* and from *sinners*...It means that his essence is pure moral goodness and is the very opposite of all evil...To say that God is holy means, positively, that he is absolute ethical perfection and purity, that he is unconditionally upright in his essence and his actions."[15]

GOD'S NAME IS HOLY

His name, which describes his nature and character, is holy. "For thus says the High and Lofty One who inhabits eternity, whose name is Holy" (Isa. 57:15; Psa. 105:3). "I am the Lord, your Holy One, the Creator of Israel, your King" (Isa. 43:15). Jesus said, "Our Father in heaven, hallowed be Your name" (Matt. 6:9). Jesus addressed his Father as "Holy Father" (Jn. 17:11). God's name should always be spoken with devout reverence for his name is set apart and above all names.

ALL ASSOCIATED WITH GOD IS HOLY

His infinite holiness is manifested in all that he is and does. "The Lord is righteous in all his ways, and holy in all his works" (Psa. 145:17 KJV). He is holy in all his attributes. Heaven is holy for he dwells there. "Look down from Your holy habitation, from heaven..." (Deut. 26:15; Isa. 57:15). His angels are holy (Mk. 8:38). His words and promises are holy (Jer. 23:9; Psa. 105:42). The priest "shall be holy" (Lev. 21:6). Because he said the Hebrew nation "shall be a special treasure to Me above all people," they were "a holy nation" (Ex. 19:5-6). His presence made the ground on which Moses stood "holy ground" (Ex. 3:5). The temple was holy "for the glory of the Lord filled the house of the Lord" (Psa. 65:4; 1 Kgs. 8:10-11). The Spirit of God is holy. David pleaded with God, "Do not cast me away from your presence, and do not take Your Holy Spirit from me" (Psa. 51:11).

JESUS IS HOLY

Peter referred to Jesus as "Holy One" in teaching that his resurrection was fulfillment of prophecy by David. "Because You will not leave my soul in Hades, nor will you allow Your Holy One to see corruption" (Acts 2:27; Psa. 16:10). Peter told the Jews that they had "denied the Holy One and the Just" (Acts 3:14). Jesus identified himself to the church at Philadelphia as "He who is holy, He who is true" (Rev. 3:7).

CHRISTIANS ARE SAINTS (HOLY)

Paul wrote, "To the church of God which is at Corinth, to those who are sanctified in Christ Jesus, called to be saints" (1 Cor. 1:2). "To sanctify anything is to declare that it belongs to God. It may refer to persons, places, days and seasons, and objects used for worship."[16]

> Sanctification is also used in N.T. of the separation of the believer from evil things and ways. This sanctification is God's will for the believer, 1 Thess. 4:3, and His purpose in calling him by the gospel, ver. 7; it must be learned from God, ver. 4, as He teaches it by His Word, Jn. 17:17, 19; cp. Ps. 17:4; 119:9, and it must be pursued by the believer, earnestly and undeviatingly, 1 Tim. 2:15; Heb. 12:14. For the holy character *hagiosune*, 1 Thess. 3:13, is not vicarious, i.e., it cannot be transferred or imputed, it is an individual possession, built up, little by little, as a result of obedience to the Word of God, and following the example of Christ...."[17]

CHRISTIANS ARE SANCTIFIED BY JESUS' BLOOD

"Therefore Jesus also, that He might sanctify the people with His own blood, suffered outside the gate" (Heb. 13:12). The blood of Jesus sanctifies us when it washes away our sins. "To Him who loved us and washed us from our sins in His own blood" (Rev. 1:5; Matt. 26:28). His precious blood washes away our sins when we are baptized. "Arise and be baptized, and wash away your sins, calling on the name of the Lord" (Acts 22:16). We are baptized into his death (Rom. 6:3). It was in his death that his blood was poured out (Jn. 19:34). Our sins are **not** washed away by his blood **before** baptism, but **in** baptism. This makes baptism **essential** to our salvation (Mk. 16:16). Having been sanctified, set apart from the world by the blood of Jesus, Christians are now "a vessel of honor, sanctified and useful for the Master" (2 Tim. 2:21) and now can one day "see the Lord" (Heb. 12:14).

GOD HATES EVIL, BUT LOVES HOLINESS

Because God is infinitely holy, he hates that which is contrary to holiness, but loves that which conforms to his holy nature. "The way of the wicked is an abomination to the Lord, but He loves him follows righteousness" (Prov. 15:8-9, 26). Proverbs 6:16-19 reveals seven things which are an abomination to him. "A proud look, a lying tongue, hands that shed innocent blood, a heart that devises wicked plans, feet that are swift in running to evil, false witness who speaks lies, and one who sows discord among the brethren." To be like their heavenly Father, Christians must "Abhor what is evil. Cling to what is good" (Rom. 12:9). "If we can learn to abhor all evil and love all that is good, we will be holy...we will be like God."[18]

CONTRAST BETWEEN GOD'S HOLINESS AND MAN'S SINFULNESS

After Isaiah saw the awesome majesty of God's holiness, he cried, "Woe is me, for I am undone! Because I am a man of unclean lips and I dwell in the midst of a people with unclean lips, for my eyes have seen the King, the Lord of hosts" (Isa. 6:5). Isaiah saw his deplorable sinfulness when in the presence of God's holiness. The filthy, polluted condition of our sinful souls comes into clear focus when we see a glimpse of God's pure holiness (Rom. 7:24).

One can be fully assured that the Bible is a product of Divine inspiration for no descendant of Adam would have invented an infinite holy God who demands that those whom he created be as holy as he is holy (1 Pet. 1:15-16). Man would have never made the terrible punishment, for failing to live a holy life, eternal torment in a lake of fire (Rev. 21:8).

CHRISTIANS MUST LIVE HOLY LIVES

Christians are: called "with a holy calling" (2 Tim. 1:9); a holy temple of God (1 Cor. 3:16-17); to offer their bodies a holy sacrifice (Rom. 12:1); "a holy priesthood" (1 Pet. 2:5); and "a holy nation" (1 Pet. 2:9).

God has promised to receive us as his "sons and daughters" if we will "come out from among them and be separate...Do not touch what is unclean...cleanse ourselves from all filthiness of the flesh and spirit, perfecting holiness in the fear of God" (2 Cor. 6:17-7:1). By inspiration, Peter wrote, "...but as He who called you is holy, you also be holy in all your conduct, because it is written, 'Be holy, for I am holy'" (1 Pet. 1:15-16; Lev. 11:44-45). Our most important goal must be to become as holy as our heavenly Father!

> Holy, holy, holy, Lord God Almighty!
> Early in the morning our song shall rise to Thee;
> Holy, holy, holy! Merciful and Mighty!
> God over all, and blest eternally.
> – *Reginald Heber*

QUESTIONS

SINCE "GOD IS SPIRIT":

1. He does not have _flesh_ and _bones_ .

2. "No one has seen _God_ at any _time_ ."

3. It is _Impossible_ for an _material image_ to look like _Him_ .

4. He is not subject to _Sickness_ , _decay_ , or _death_ .

5. He is not confined to one _place_ .

FILL IN THE BLANK AND GIVE THE SCRIPTURE

1. "_God_ is _Spirit_ ... must worship in _Spirit_ and _truth_ " (_John 4:24_)

2. "For _I_ am _God_ , and not _man_ " (_Hos 11:9_)

3. "God is not a _man_ , that _He_ should _lie_ " (_Num 23:19_

4. "...we ought not to _____ that the _____ _____ is like _____ , or _____ , or _____ " (_____)

5. "The _____ of the _____ are in every _____ " (_____)

6. "..._He_ is not far from _each_ one of _us_ " (_Acts 17:27_

7. "_Holy_ , _Holy_ , _Holy_ , is the _God_ of hosts" (_Isa 6:3_

8. "For thus says the _High_ and _lofty One_ ...whose name is _Holy_ " (_Isa 57:15_)

9. "The _____ is _____ in all His _____ , and _____ in all His _____ " (_____ KJV)

10. "Be _____ for ____ am _____" (_____)

TRUE OR FALSE

1. _F_ God was once a man who evolved into God.

2. _F_ God created our physical bodies like his body.

3. _T_ We will be raised with a spiritual body.

4. _T_ Man is unable to see spirits.

5. _F_ Some material images are not corruptible.

6. _F_ One can hide from God.

7. _T_ Holy is the only attribute of God repeated three times in succession.

8. _T_ Something is holy if it is separated for God's use.

9. _T_ Jesus is called the "Holy One."

10. _F_ One can be a Christian, but not a saint.

FILL IN THE BLANKS

1. Who said, "God is not a man that He should lie"? _Balaam_

2. _Anthropomorphism_ is a figure of speech ascribing human characteristics to God.

3. The worship of _idolatry_ is condemned in both testaments.

4. Holiness is a great difference between _____ and _____.

5. Who said, "There is none holy like the Lord"? _____

6. Jesus addressed his Father as "_Holy_ _Father_."

7. Christians are _____ by Jesus' _____ when they are
   _____.

8. Christians must "_____ what is evil. Cling to what is
   _____."

9. Who said, "Woe is me for I am undone"? _____

10. Our most important goal should be to become as _____ as
    _____.

THOUGHT QUESTIONS

1. Name some things that God hates.

2. How do we know that man did not write the Bible?

3. What must we do for God to receive us as his "sons and daughters"?

GOD IS
LOVE, LIGHT, & TRUTH

GOD IS LOVE

"Beloved, let us love one another, for love is of God; and everyone who loves is born of God and knows God. He who does not love does not know God, for God is love… And we have known and believed the love that God has for us. God is love, and he who abides in love abides in God, and God in him" (1 Jn. 4:7, 8, 16). Love originates in God and proceeds from him.

"The Bible makes the unique revelation that God in His very nature and essence is love (1 Jn. 4:8, 16), Christianity being the only religion thus to present the Supreme Being. God not only loves, He *is* love. In this supreme attribute all the other attributes are harmonized."[1] "In response to man's sin-caused misery and suffering, love takes the form of mercy. In response to man's persistence in sin, it shows itself as patience. And in response to the sinner's condemnation and lostness, it becomes forgiving grace."[2]

DEFINITION OF LOVE

Love is defined as, "A strong, complex emotion or feeling causing to appreciate, delight in, and crave the presence or possession of another and to please and promote the welfare of another; devoted affection or attachment."[3] The International Standard Bible Encyclopedia gives this definition of love, "Love, whether used of God or man, is an earnest and anxious desire for, and an active and beneficent interest in, the well-being of the one loved."[4] God's definition of love is recorded in 1 Corinthians 13:4-7.

HOW WONDERFUL THAT GOD IS LOVE!

The most wonderful news that man can receive is that God is love. (1 John 4:16) God is eternal. But if He is not concerned for man who is a creature of time, a created being who thus has not existed eternally, then man can have no real and lasting hope. God is all powerful, but if God does not love man, the power of God becomes simply a source of terror to us. God is holy; but if God does not love us the holiness of God must repel us from God, for we are unholy. God is just, but we have sinned and, unless there is compassion with God, there is only fear in the heart of man when he thinks upon the holiness of God and of man's own sinfulness. Thus without the truth that God is love, the other truths about God, would work for our condemnation and not for our salvation.[5]

God's being omnipresent would not comfort us, but terrify us if he was cruel and mean for there would be no place for us to hide from his fierce wrath. (Psa. 139). How thankful we should be that our Creator is not like the gods (idols) of man's imagination! They were not kind, loving, merciful, gracious, holy, etc. We should greatly rejoice and wholeheartedly praise God for his immeasurable love for us.

THE SUPREME EXPRESSION OF LOVE

"For God so loved the world that He gave His only begotten Son that whoever believes in Him should not perish but have everlasting life" (Jn. 3:16). Because of God's infinite love for us, he took the initiative in providing a way for sin to be removed from our souls. His plan for our salvation from eternal torment involved the agonizing death of "His only begotten Son" on a cross. He loved his "beloved Son" (Matt. 3:17) "before the foundation of the world" (Jn. 17:24). His Son begged him "with vehement cries and tears" (Heb. 5:7) to provide another way for removing sin from man's soul. "O My Father, if it is possible, let this cup pass from Me; nevertheless, not as I will, but as You will" (Matt. 26:39). However, only "the precious blood of Christ, as of a lamb without blemish" (1 Pet. 1:19) could atone for man's sins (Matt. 26:28).

THE UNQUESTIONABLE LOVE GOD HAS FOR US

The "Angel of the Lord" stopped Abraham from sacrificing his son, Isaac (Gen. 22:11, 12). No one stopped the Father from sacrificing his Son for us. How could anyone ever doubt his unfathomable love for us? "This is love: not that we loved God, but that he loved us and sent his Son as an atoning sacrifice for our sins" (1 Jn. 4:10 New International Version).

How could anyone ever question Christ's great love for us? "By this we know love because He laid down His life for us. And we also ought to lay down our lives for the brethren" (1 Jn. 3:16). "Greater love has no one than this, than to lay down one's life for his friends" (Jn. 15:13).

GOD LOVES SINFUL MAN
"But God demonstrates His own love toward us, in that while we were still sinners, Christ died for us. Much more then, having now been justified by His blood, we shall be saved from wrath through Him. For if when we were enemies we were reconciled to God through the death of His Son, much more, having been reconciled, we shall be saved by His life" (Rom. 5:8-10).

God's love is so great that he loves corrupt, rebellious, sinful humans. "In respect of *agapao* as used of God, it expresses the deep and constant love and interest of a perfect Being towards entirely unworthy objects, producing and fostering a reverential love in them towards the Giver and a practical love toward those who are partakers of the same, and a desire to help others to seek the Giver."[6] It is easy and natural to love those that are kind, sweet, respectful, etc. but extremely difficult to love one's enemies (Matt. 5:43-48). However, God loves the "world" (Jn. 3:16) and Jesus died "for everyone" (Heb. 2:9).

GOD LOVES EACH ONE OF US
"The God who marks the death of a sparrow and who knows the names and numbers of the stars and of the hairs of our head certainly loves you and me as individuals and not solely as a drop in the sea of humanity."[7] Paul wrote, "I live by faith in the Son of God, who loved me and gave Himself for me" (Gal. 2:20). It is a great comfort to know that our Lord knows and cares about you and me (1 Pet. 5:7)! "He is not far from each one of us" (Acts 17:27). "Jesus loves me! this I know, For the Bible tells me so; Little ones to Him belong; They are weak but He is strong" (Anna B. Warner).

GOD PROVES HIS LOVE FOR US
"He makes His sun rise on the evil and the good, and sends rain on the just and on the unjust" (Matt. 5:45). Without sunshine and rain, plant and animal life could not exist. Paul told the people of Lystra, "Nevertheless He did not leave Himself without witness, in that He did good, gave us

rain from heaven and fruitful seasons, filling our hearts with food and gladness" (Acts 14:17).

Because of his love for us, he wants to forgive our sins. "But You are God, ready to pardon" (Neh. 9:17). "For I will be merciful to their unrighteousness and their sins and their lawless deeds I will remember no more" (Heb. 8:12). When you love someone, you want to forgive them so that the hurt feelings will be replaced with feelings of affection.

Because of his wonderful love for us, he: knows and supplies our needs (Matt. 6:8; Phil. 4:19); gives "good things to those who ask Him" (Matt. 7:11); is the source of "every good gift and every perfect gift" (Jas. 1:17); gives us mercy and "grace to help in time of need" (Heb. 4:16); and calls us his children (1 Jn. 3:1). How can anyone refuse to love and worship him?

CHRISTIANS MUST SINCERELY LOVE GOD
"'You shall love the Lord your God with all your heart, with all your soul, and with all your mind.' This is the first and great commandment" (Matt. 22:37, 38). "As love is the highest expression of God and His relation to mankind, so it must be the highest expression of man's relation to his Maker and to his fellow-man."[8] We must love God more than: any person (Matt. 10:37); any possession (Lk. 14:33); and our lives (Matt. 10:39). We may profess to really love God, but we prove it by keeping his commandments (Jn. 14:15, 21-24). If we love the Lord, we will not forsake our assembling with the saints (Heb. 10:25), but be present to worship him. It is a privilege to worship God!

CHRISTIANS MUST LOVE THEIR BROTHER
"If someone says, 'I love God,' and hates his brother, he is a liar; for he who does not love his brother whom he has seen, how can he love God whom he has not seen? And this commandment we have from Him: that he who loves God must love his brother also" (1 Jn. 4:20-21). We show our love for God by loving his children (Matt. 25:34-40). The word of God teaches us to have a "sincere love of the brethren, love one another fervently with a pure heart" (1 Pet. 1:22). We show to others that we are the Lord's disciples by loving one another to the same degree that he loves us (Jn. 13:34, 35). Our love for the brethren is what motivates us to "serve one another" (Gal. 5:13). If we hate our brother, we are "a murderer" and have lost "eternal life" (1 Jn. 3:15).

CHRISTIANS MUST LOVE THEIR NEIGHBOR
"And the second is like it: 'You shall love your neighbor as yourself.' On these two commandments hang all the Law and the Prophets" (Matt. 22:39, 40). If you "love your neighbor as yourself," you will not harm him, but treat him in a just, honest, kind manner. You will practice the golden rule (Matt. 7:12). You will teach him: about the marvelous love of God; how to receive the forgiveness one's sins; and what to do to live with the blessed hope of eternal life in heaven. Jesus taught that our neighbor is anyone we meet (Lk. 10:25-37).

CHRISTIANS MUST LOVE THEIR ENEMIES
"But I say to you, love your enemies, bless those who curse you, do good to those who hate you, and pray for those who spitefully use you and persecute you, that you may be sons of your Father in heaven" (Matt. 5:44, 45). Jesus has given us an amazing example of what it means to love our enemies. He said, while dying an agonizing death on the cross, "Father, forgive them, for they do not know what they do" (Lk. 23:34). How can we profess to be his disciples when we hate and afflict those who hate and afflict us? We must rise above the standard of the world (Matt. 5:46-48).

"THE GREATEST OF THESE IS LOVE"
"Now abide faith, hope, love, these three; but the greatest of these is love" (1 Cor. 13:13). If our work for the Lord is not motivated by love, it profits us nothing (1 Cor. 13:1-3). All that we do must "be done with love" (1 Cor. 16:14). Our love for God, brethren, neighbor, and enemies must "be without hypocrisy" (Rom. 12:9).

GOD IS LIGHT
"This is the message which we have heard from Him and declare to you, that God is light and in Him is no darkness at all" (1 Jn. 1:5). "The affirmation, 'God is light,' is not the same as 'God is the light' or 'God is a light,' but simply God is light, such is his essence; he is of the character of light. The word 'light' sums up the divine character on the intellectual side, as 'God is love,' similarly describes the fullness of his moral nature."[9] God is the source of light (Jas. 1:17). The Father and Son are the eternal light in heaven (Rev. 21:23; 22:5). His first recorded words are, "Let there be light" (Gen. 1:3). The creation of light before the creation of plant and animal life was essential for organic life to live.

"IN HIM IS NO DARKNESS AT ALL"

"If we say that we have fellowship with Him, and walk in darkness, we lie and do not practice the truth. But if we walk in the light as He is in the light, we have fellowship with one another, and the blood of Jesus Christ His Son cleanses us from all sin" (1 Jn. 1:6, 7).

> 'Darkness' is a figure of ignorance, superstition, and sin, as 'light' represents truth, purity, and goodness. In this manner, God is contrasted with the heathen deities the worship of which promoted immorality, ungodliness, and gross sin. The devil and his agents are styled 'the world rulers of this darkness' (Eph. 6:12), and their domain is called 'the power of darkness' (Col. 1:13). Those formerly enmeshed in the mazes of heathenism were said to have been 'once darkness,' but now as a result of their obedience to the gospel, 'light in the Lord.' (Eph. 5:8).[10]

Those, who claim to have fellowship with God but are not obeying his commandments, are liars. We can only have fellowship with him by walking in compliance with his teaching for then we are walking "in the light" (1 Jn. 1:7). Our profession and practice must be in agreement.

JESUS IS "THE LIGHT OF THE WORLD"

Jesus said, "I am the light of the world. He who follows Me shall not walk in darkness, but have the light of life" (Jn. 8:12; 9:5). Just as sunlight is essential to life on earth so Jesus is essential to spiritual life. "In Him was life, and the life was the light of men" (Jn. 1:4). Unlike sunlight, which shines upon all, the light Jesus gives only helps those who will look to him for instruction. Sadly, many will not allow him to be their light for they love "darkness rather than light" (Jn. 3:19). They love darkness because their works are evil and they do not want them to "be exposed" (Jn. 3:19-21). These have no direction or purpose in life for they do not know where they are going (Jn. 12:35-36). They are lost "like sheep having no shepherd" (Matt. 9:36). How sad for a person to be physically blind, but is far worse to be spiritually blind! Many are following blind spiritual guides to their eternal destruction (Matt. 15:14).

GOD'S WORD IS LIGHT

"Your word is a lamp to my feet and a light to my path...The entrance of Your word gives light; it gives understanding to the simple" (Psa. 119:105, 130). "For the commandment is a lamp and the law is light" (Prov. 6:23). God's word is light for it gives wisdom, knowledge, and understanding to those who will read and believe it (Psa. 119:104). It will enlighten us in many important truths far above what any uninspired book can do (Psa. 119:98-100). If we will meditate on it and live by its teaching, it will remove ignorance, superstition, and give us strength to say "No" to temptation (Psa. 119:9; Matt. 4:1-11).

It produces faith in Jesus as God's Son and that faith moves us to obey him and thus become "sons of light" (Jn. 12:36). Jesus sent Paul to the Gentiles "to open their eyes and turn them from darkness to light and from the power of Satan to God" (Acts 26:17, 18). Paul accomplished these wonderful results by preaching the gospel so "the light of the gospel of the glory of Christ, who is the image of God, should shine on them" (2 Cor. 4:4).

CHRISTIANS ARE "THE LIGHT OF THE WORLD"
"You are the light of the world...Let your light so shine before men, that they may see your good works and glorify your Father in heaven" (Matt. 5:14-16). We "walk as children of light" when we reflect the "light in the Lord...and have no fellowship with the unfruitful works of darkness" (Eph. 5:8-11). We are letting our lights shine in this dark world of sin by "holding fast the word of life" (Phil. 2:14-16). How thankful we should be that God has called us by the gospel (2 Thess. 2:14) "out of darkness into His marvelous light" (1 Pet. 2:9) "to be partakers of the inheritance of the saints in the light" (Col. 1:12)! If we are not "sons of light," who are "walking in the light," we have no inheritance with the "saints in the light."

GOD IS TRUTH
Moses sang, "He is the Rock, His work is perfect; for His ways are justice, a God of truth and without injustice; righteous and upright is He" (Deut. 32:4). The Lord gives this description of himself to Moses, "The Lord, the Lord God, merciful and gracious, longsuffering and abounding in goodness and truth" (Ex. 34:6). Jesus said of his Father, "He who sent Me is true" (Jn. 7:28). Jesus called his Father "the only true God" (Jn. 17:3). Paul commended the Thessalonian brethren for turning "to God from idols to serve the living and true God" (1 Thess. 1:9). Idols are lifeless, false gods that are made with men's hands and not able to speak, see, hear, smell, walk, etc. (Psa. 115:4-8)

GOD CANNOT LIE
"...in hope of eternal life which God, who cannot lie, promised before time began" (Tit. 1:2). The writer of Hebrews states, "it is impossible for

God to lie" (6:18). Balaam said, "God is not a man, that He should lie" (Num. 23:19). Since "it is impossible for God to lie, then his: "commandments are truth" (Psa. 119:151); judgments are according to truth (Psa. 96:13); and "word is truth" (Jn. 17:17). We can have full assurance that all that God has said is trustworthy! If man teaches anything which disagrees with what God has said, then man is teaching a lie (Rom. 3:4).

GOD HATES LYING!

Because God is the essence of truth, he abhors lying for it is contrary to his holy nature. Consider that two of the seven things that "are an abomination to Him" are "a lying tongue" and "a false witness who speaks lies" (Prov. 6:16-19). A liar "will not escape," but "shall perish" (Prov. 19:5, 9). The horrible, eternal consequence of lying is clearly revealed in Revelation 21:8, "...all liars shall have their part in the lake which burns with fire and brimstone, which is the second death." If we tell a lie, we must repent and diligently seek God's forgiveness!

JESUS IS TRUTH

"And the Word became flesh and dwelt among us, and we beheld His glory, the glory of the only begotten of the Father, full of grace and truth... For the law was given through Moses, but grace and truth came through Jesus Christ" (Jn. 1:14, 17). Jesus said, "I am the way, the truth, and the life. No one comes to the Father except through Me" (Jn. 14:6). Even the enemies of Jesus confessed, "Teacher, we know that You are true and teach the way of God in truth" (Matt. 22:16). Why did not these enemies believe in him? They did not want to be identified as his disciples. None so blind as those who will not see. If we believe what these said about Jesus, then we should gladly be his disciples and abide in his word that we may "know the truth" which will free us from ignorance and the bondage of sin (Jn. 8:31, 32). Jesus is the "good shepherd" who will lead us safely to heaven (Jn. 10:11, 27, 28).

HOLY SPIRIT IS TRUTH

"However, when He, the Spirit of truth, has come, He will guide you into all truth" (Jn. 16:13). The Holy Spirit came upon the apostles the first Pentecost after Jesus' resurrection (Acts 2:1-4). He revealed "all truth" to them (Jude 3). All latter day revelations have been written by uninspired men and women and must not be accepted as truth!

CHRISTIAN'S ATTITUDE TOWARD TRUTH

Christians must: "serve Him in sincerity and truth" (Josh. 24:14); "worship in spirit and truth" (Jn. 4:24); speak "the truth in love" (Eph. 4:15); and have a "love of the truth" to be saved (2 Thess. 2:10). We must never turn our "ears away from the truth, and be turned aside to fables" (2 Tim. 4:4). Do you love the truth?

QUESTIONS

1. What is the supreme expression of love? _____
   _____
   _____

2. What is the only thing precious enough to remove sin from man's soul?
   _____
   _____

3. Who stopped Abraham from sacrificing Isaac? _____
   _____

4. Name some beneficial things God's love does for us. _____
   _____
   _____

5. You should love God with all your what? _____
   _____
   _____

6. You should love your neighbor as what? _____
   _____
   _____

7. How do we prove our love for God? _____
   _____

8. What does the Bible call you if you say you love God, but hate your brother? _____
   _____

9. If you love your neighbor, you will practice what? _____
_____
_____

10. If we love our enemies, what will we do for them? _____
_____
_____

11. What does the Bible call those who claim to be in fellowship with God, but "walk in darkness? _____
_____

12. Why do some love "darkness"? _____
_____

13. Who called God the "God of truth"? _____
_____

14. What can God not do? _____
_____
_____

FILL IN THE BLANK AND GIVE THE SCRIPTURE

1. "For _____ so loved the _____ that He _____ His only begotten _____" (_____)

2. "Greater _____ has no _____ than this, than to _____ down one's _____ for his _____" (_____)

3. "…while we were still _____, Christ _____ for us" (_____)

4. "I live by _____ in the _____ of _____, who _____ me and gave _____ for _____" (_____)

5. "He is not _____ from each _____ of us" (_____)

6. "He makes His _____ rise on the _____ and on the _____" (_____)

7. "But You are _____, ready to _____" (_____)

8. "God is _____ and in _____ is no _____ at all" (_____)

9. "I am the _____ of the _____" (_____)

10. "Your word is a _____ to my _____ and a _____ to my _____" (_____)

11. "...light of the _____ of the glory of _____, who is the _____ of God" (_____)

12. "The Lord, the Lord _____, _____ and _____, _____ and abounding in _____ and _____" (_____)

13. "...who called _____ out of _____ into _____ marvelous _____" (_____)

14. "...all _____ shall have their part in the _____ which _____ with _____ and _____" (_____)

THOUGHT QUESTIONS

1. How do Christians let their light shine?

2. Why do you believe God's word is absolute truth?

THE MERCY, GRACE, AND LONGSUFFERING OF GOD

The Lord God described himself as "merciful and gracious, longsuffering, and abounding in goodness and truth, keeping mercy for thousands, forgiving iniquity and transgression and sin..." (Ex. 34:6-7). These great characteristics reveal much about God's true nature, and account for his actions toward man throughout history. They are worthy of our study that we may understand our God and emulate his holy character in our own lives. This lesson will consider the mercy, grace, and longsuffering of God.

THE MERCY OF GOD

The English word "mercy" means "a refraining from harming or punishing offenders, enemies, persons in one's power, etc.; kindness in excess of what may be expected or demanded by fairness; forebearance and compassion."[1] When we speak of the mercy (Heb. *hesed*; Gk. *eleos*) of God we speak mainly of his compassion, or pity, upon those who are helpless. This word in the New Testament

> ...describes the emotional response and resulting action after encountering the suffering or affliction of another: "to have mercy, feel sorry for, have pity." It is used particularly of God's mercy: giving undeserved kindness or forgiveness to those who do not deserve it.[2]

SCRIPTURAL DECLARATIONS OF GOD'S MERCY

The following passages describe the fullness and splendor of the mercy of God:

"I am in great distress. Please let us fall into the hand of the Lord, for His mercies are great" (2 Sam. 24:14).

"Lord God of Israel, there is no God in heaven above or on earth below like You who keep Your covenant and mercy with Your servants who walk before You with all their heart" (1 Kgs. 8:23).

"For the Lord is good; His mercy is everlasting" (Psa. 100:5).

"Praise the Lord! Oh, give thanks to the Lord, for He is good! For His mercy endures forever" (Psa. 106:1).

"The earth, O Lord, is full of Your mercy" (Psa. 119:64).

"Who is a God like You...He does not retain His anger forever because He delights in mercy. He will again have compassion on us, and will subdue our iniquities" (Micah 7:18, 19).

"And His mercy is on those who fear Him from generation to generation" (Lk. 1:50).

"Blessed be the God and Father of our Lord Jesus Christ, the Father of mercies and God of all comfort" (2 Cor. 1:3).

"...the Lord is very compassionate and merciful" (Jas. 5:11).

GOD'S MERCY AND MAN'S SALVATION

Mankind should be very thankful for the abundant mercies of God, since "all have sinned and fall short of the glory of God" (Rom. 3:23). As sinners, we are in a most pitiful condition before a holy God. The sinner is helpless to remedy his condition that will result in eternal separation from God. Man's only hope was that God would look upon sinners with mercy, and provide a way of salvation. We can rejoice that our God is full of mercy toward us to save us (cf. 1 Tim. 1:13)! "But God, who is rich in mercy, because of His great love with which He loved us, even when we were dead in trespasses, made us alive together with Christ" (Eph. 2:4-5).

The mercy of God is extended to man because of God's great love. He is merciful because he is loving. There can never be a genuine expression of mercy without there first being the love for the one who needs mercy. God is love, therefore God is merciful to all, for God loves all men (Jn. 3:16).

The apostle Paul combines the characteristics of love, grace, and mercy as he writes about our salvation in Christ:

But when the kindness and the love of God our Savior toward man appeared, not by works of righteousness which we have done, but according to His mercy He saved us, through the washing of regeneration and renewing of the Holy Spirit, whom He poured out on us abundantly through Jesus Christ our Savior, that having been justified by His grace we should become heirs according to the hope of eternal life (Tit. 3:4-7).

The new covenant of Christ is where God's mercy is expressed in its fullness. When God announced the coming of the new covenant, he declared, "For I will be merciful to their unrighteousness, and their sins and their lawless deeds I will remember no more" (Heb. 8:12). The mercy of God continues to be available to all who are in covenant with God through Christ: "Let us therefore come boldly to the throne of grace, that we may obtain mercy and find grace to help in time of need" (Heb. 4:16).[3]

WE ARE TO BE MERCIFUL LIKE OUR GOD

As children of God, Christians are to show mercy. Israel of old was shown "what is good; and what does the Lord require of you but to do justly, *to love mercy*, and to walk humbly with your God" (Micah 6:8). Jesus taught us how to be merciful like the heavenly Father: "But love your enemies, do good, and lend, hoping for nothing in return; and your reward will be great, and you will be sons of the Most High. For He is kind to the unthankful and evil. Therefore be merciful, just as your Father also is merciful" (Lk. 6:35-36). If we show no mercy, we should expect no mercy from God. "For judgment is without mercy to the one who has shown no mercy. Mercy triumphs over judgment" (Jas. 2:13). Why would anyone rejoice in receiving the mercy of God, and then refuse to extend godly mercy to those truly in need around them? The parable of the unmerciful servant shows us how important it is to God that we extend the same mercy he extends to us (Matt. 18:21-35). Let us be merciful, kind people in this wicked world. "The Lord takes pleasure in those who fear Him, in those who hope in His mercy" (Psa. 147:11).

THE GRACE OF GOD

There are few subjects as wondrous as the grace of God. There are also few subjects as misunderstood and misapplied as the grace of God. Grace (Gk. *charis*) is defined as "that which bestows or occasions pleasure, delight, or causes favourable regard"[4]; "the acceptance of and goodness toward those who cannot earn or do not deserve such gain."[5] A popular definition is "unmerited favor," that is, favor that is unearned, but extended out of love. "It is God showing goodness to persons who deserve only severity and had no reason to expect anything but severity."[6] Our God is declared to be the "God of all grace, who called us to His eternal glory by Christ Jesus..." (1 Pet. 5:10).

SAVED BY GRACE

Salvation from sin has been brought to man by the grace of God (Tit. 2:11). This salvation by grace is fully discussed by Paul in the following passage:

> And you He made alive, who were dead in trespasses and sins, in which you once walked according to the course of this world, according to the prince of the power of the air, the spirit who now works in the sons of disobedience, among whom also we all once conducted ourselves in the lusts of our flesh, fulfilling the desires of the flesh and of the mind, and were by nature children of wrath, just as the others. But God, who is rich in mercy, because of His great love with which He loved us, even when we were dead in trespasses, made us alive together with Christ (by grace you have been saved), and raised us up together, and made us sit together in the heavenly places in Christ Jesus, that in the ages to come He might show the exceeding riches of His grace in His kindness to- ward us in Christ Jesus. For by grace you have been saved through faith, and that not of yourselves; it is the gift of God, not of works, lest anyone should boast. For we are His workmanship, created in Christ Jesus for good works, which God prepared beforehand that we should walk in them (Eph. 2:1-10).

This passage clearly teaches that we have been saved by grace, but *not* grace alone. Salvation is by grace through faith. Grace is God's part and faith is man's part. Grace is extended by God to sinful man, and faith is the necessary response of man by obedience.[7] We are not saved by grace alone, nor by faith alone, but by grace through faith.

Faith is the *means* by which the grace of God (which provides salvation) is accessed by man. "Therefore, having been justified by faith, we have peace with God through our Lord Jesus Christ, through whom also we have *access by faith into this grace* in which we stand, and rejoice in hope of the glory of God" (Rom. 5:1-2).

The grace of God is seen and demonstrated in the gift of Christ Jesus who gave his life to save man from sin. "But God demonstrates His own love toward us, in that while we were still sinners, Christ died for us" (Rom. 5:8). Jesus, in his love and sacrifice for us, embodies the grace of God extended to all who come to him. Those who refuse the Father's call by the gospel to be "justified freely by His grace through the redemption that is in Christ Jesus" (Rom. 3:24), will be judged as those who have "insulted the Spirit of grace" (Heb. 10:29).

Not Under Law, but Under Grace

"For sin shall not have dominion over you, for you are not under law but under grace" (Rom. 6:14). This passage has been misunderstood to say that we are "free" to believe and act as we wish, and there is no doctrinal law that we are required to follow to be pleasing to God. The fact is we are under the law of Christ (Gal. 6:2; Jas. 1:25). What we are *not* under is a system of "perfect law-keeping" justification. "The law of works described a system of justification based on perfect obedience to the expressed and binding will of God. Should that be accomplished, it would be a matter not of grace, but of debt (Rom. 4:4)."[8] This system of law justification offers no hope because all men have sinned (Rom. 3:23).

Thankfully, we know that "a man is not justified by the works of the law but by faith in Jesus Christ, even we have believed in Christ Jesus, that we might be justified by faith in Christ and not by the works of the law, for by the works of the law no flesh shall be justified" (Gal. 2:16). Under the covenant and law of Christ, we have salvation by grace through faith where the perfect blood of Christ is always available to cleanse us from all unrighteousness (1 Jn. 1:7, 9). This is what it means to be "under grace" and every Christian can say, "By the grace of God I am what I am" (1 Cor. 15:10).

Continual Access to Divine Grace

The Christian has the wonderful blessing of continual access to the grace of God.

> Seeing then that we have a great High Priest who has passed through the heavens, Jesus the Son of God, let us hold fast our confession. For we do not have a High Priest who cannot sympathize with our weaknesses, but was in all points tempted as we are, yet without sin. Let us therefore come boldly to the throne of grace, that we may obtain mercy and find grace to help in time of need (Heb. 4:14-16).

The admonition to "come boldly" is in the present tense which "emphasizes that the privilege is always available."[9]

We also are continually taught by the grace of God: "For the grace of God that brings salvation has appeared to all men, teaching us that, denying ungodliness and worldly lusts, we should live soberly, righteously, and godly in the present age" (Tit. 2:11-12). God's grace teaches us by means of the revealed will of God. God graciously revealed his mind to us by the Spirit through the apostles and prophets of the new covenant (Eph. 3:3-5). We need to listen closely to the teaching of the grace of God in the complete, all-sufficient word of truth, avoiding sin, and living so as to please God. Let us be careful to not "set aside the grace of God" (Gal. 2:21), but to stand firmly in the "true grace of God" (1 Pet. 5:12).

THE LONGSUFFERING OF GOD

The longsuffering of God is a fascinating and encouraging subject. The concept of "longsuffering" (Gk. *makrothymia*) is the same as "patience." God demonstrated patient longsuffering in the days of Noah while the ark was being built (1 Pet. 3:20). William Mounce explains further the concept of the patience of God:

> God's patience must not be underestimated. Because he is patient with us, he does not treat us as we deserve; thus, we do not perish. Reflecting on these things, the psalmist writes, "The Lord is compassionate and gracious, slow to anger, abounding in love. He will not always accuse, nor will he harbor his anger forever; he does not treat us as our sins deserve or repay us according to our iniquities" (Ps. 103:8-10).[10]

> "From macros, "long" (in terms of time), and thymos, "the soul" as the seat of feelings and passions (including anger, temper)... "to be long of feeling, delay one's anger" (as in "longsuffering")... Patience is first of all a quality of God. He shows his patience in that he wishes everyone to repent (2 Pet. 3:9) and be saved (3:15), so that he delays punishment (Rom. 2:4), as in Paul's case (1 Tim. 1:16). God's patience provides the extra time sometimes needed to bring someone to repentance....[11]

Hogg and Vine add the following:

> Longsuffering is that quality of self-restraint in the face of provocation which does not hastily retaliate or promptly punish; it is the opposite of anger, and is associated with mercy, and is used of God, Ex. 34:6 (Sept.), Rom. 2:4, 1 Pet. 3:20.[12]

Longsuffering (or "slow to anger") is most often joined together with mercy, grace, and kindness in Old Testament descriptions of God's character:

"The Lord is longsuffering and abundant in mercy, forgiving iniquity and transgressions..." (Num. 14:18).

"But You are God, ready to pardon, gracious and merciful, slow to anger, abundant in kindness..." (Neh. 9:17).

"The Lord is merciful and gracious, slow to anger, and abounding in mercy" (Psa. 103:8).

"So rend your heart and not your garments; return to the Lord your God, for He is gracious and merciful, slow to anger, and of great kindness; and He relents from doing harm" (Joel 2:13)

"...for I know that You are a gracious and merciful God, slow to anger and abundant in lovingkindness, One who relents from doing harm" (Jon. 4:2).

God's Longsuffering and Our Salvation

The apostle Peter wrote that "the longsuffering of our Lord is salvation" (2 Pet. 3:15). It is salvation because it provides time for man to repent of sin and prepare for the coming of the Lord. "The Lord is not slack concerning His promise, as some count slackness, but is longsuffering toward us, not willing that any should perish but that all should come to repentance" (v. 9; Rom. 2:4).

God patiently waits today for more to respond to the call of the gospel. He desires all men to be saved (1 Tim. 2:4; Mk. 16:15). How long he will wait no man knows, but his longsuffering is not eternal. Someday he will destroy this physical realm and usher in eternity – heaven for the faithful, and hell for the wicked (2 Pet. 3:10-13; Matt. 25:46).

The Christian is to be Longsuffering

Longsuffering is one of the fruits of the Spirit (Gal. 5:22). The Christian is to develop the characteristic of longsuffering in his life and to practice it (Col. 1:11; 3:12). It is part of the "walk worthy of the calling with which you were called" (Eph. 4:1-2). The evangelist is to "preach the word... convince, rebuke, exhort, with all longsuffering and teaching" (2 Tim. 4:2). It is through "faith and patience" that we will inherit the promises (Heb. 6:12). Good examples of such patience are Paul (2 Cor. 6:6; 2 Tim. 3:10) and the prophets (Jas. 5:10). We need to maintain such patience as we await our Lord's return (vv. 7-8).

We need to be patient with ourselves and one another. Too often we expect too much of ourselves and others. True love is characterized by longsuffering (1 Cor. 13:4). Modern marriages, churches, friendships, workplaces, etc. need large doses of love and longsuffering. We are too quick to "up and quit" or write somebody off as a lost cause, when time and growth can work wonders in spiritual relationships and service to the Lord. If the Lord had as little longsuffering as we often exhibit, no one would ever be found worthy of his love and salvation. In fact, man would have been wiped from this earth long ago (Gen. 6:5-7). Thankfully, God searches for those who will find grace in his eyes (v. 8). Let us heed and apply the exhortation to "warn those who are unruly, comfort the faint-hearted, uphold the weak, *be patient with all*" (1 Thess. 5:14).

CONCLUSION

Without the mercy, grace, and longsuffering of God, our great salvation never would have appeared. Our God is a great God, and we can rejoice in that he is great in mercy, gracious to us all, and longsuffering, not will-ing that any should perish. If anyone does perish, it will not be because a patient and merciful God did not provide full salvation freely by his grace. May our lips sound forth the beautiful refrain:

> The Lord is gracious and full of compassion,
> Slow to anger and great in mercy.
> The Lord is good to all,
> And His tender mercies are over all His works
> (Psa. 145:8-9).

QUESTIONS

1. What is meant by the "mercy" of God? _____
_____

2. What condition is the sinner before God? _____
_____

3. What is the sinner's only hope? _____
_____

4. Why is God's love vital to his mercy? _____
_____

5. Why should we show mercy, and to whom? _____
_____
_____

6. Give a definition of "grace." _____
_____
_____

7. How do we access the grace of God? _____
_____
_____

8. How did God demonstrate his grace to man? _____
_____

9. Where can we find our continual access to God's grace? _____
_____

10. What is another word for the concept of "longsuffering"? _____
_____

11. How is God's longsuffering involved in our salvation? _____
_____
_____

12. How can longsuffering help the Christian today? _____
_____
_____

FILL IN THE BLANK AND GIVE THE SCRIPTURE

1. "For the Lord is _____; His mercy is _____"
   (_____)
2. "For by _____ have you been _____ through faith"
   (_____)

3. "…for you are not under _____ but under grace" (_____)

4. "The Lord is… _____ toward us, not willing that any should perish but that all should come to _____" (_____)

5. "…warn those who are _____, comfort the _____, uphold the _____, be _____ with all" (_____)

TRUE OR FALSE

1. ____ We should extend mercy only toward those who are thankful and good
2. ____ We are saved by the grace of God alone, without any conditions of obedience
3. ____ Both a non-Christian and a Christian can "insult" the Spirit of grace
4. ____ A sinner can be justified by perfect law-keeping
5. ____ God's grace is only available on Sundays from 9 am to 7 pm
6. ____ God's longsuffering will eventually end
7. ____ Preachers need to use longsuffering in their work of preaching

THOUGHT QUESTIONS

1. What are the differences and similarities between mercy and grace?

2. Explain what it means that we are "not under law but under grace" (Rom. 6:14).

3. Why is it so important to develop longsuffering as part of the character of a Christian? What areas of life will be affected?

THE GOODNESS, COMPASSION, FORGIVENESS, AND IMMUTABILITY OF GOD

A children's prayer begins, "God is great, God is good...." Indeed, even a child can understand how wonderful it is to have a God that is "abounding in goodness and truth, keeping mercy for thousands, forgiving iniquity and transgression and sin..." (Ex. 34:6-7). All of God's characteristics are wondrous and thrill the soul of the believer, and some bring particular comfort to the soul. In this lesson, several comforting characteristics of God will be considered: his *goodness, compassion, forgiveness,* and *immutability.*

THE GOODNESS OF GOD

We serve a God that is full of goodness, and fills the earth with his goodness: "He loves righteousness and justice; the earth is full of the goodness of the Lord" (Psa. 33:5). "Goodness" (*chrestotes*) indicates that which is "upright, righteous" expressing itself in "grace and tenderness and compassion...Lightfoot regards *chrestotes* as a kindly disposition towards others."[1] Goodness, therefore, describes the gracious and tender disposition of God. It is comforting to know that the all-powerful and all-knowing Creator is a good and loving God. In fact, he sets the standard of what is good (Mk. 10:17-18). All that which is opposed to God and his will is intrinsically evil.

IN CREATION

We see the goodness of God from his very first act – the creation of heaven and earth. When God finished the creation it is said that he "saw everything that He had made, and indeed it was very good" (Gen. 1:31). It was "very good" because it was created by him who is good and does good (Psa. 119:68).

The original Saxon meaning of our English word "God" is "The Good." God is not only the Greatest of all beings, but the Best. All the goodness there is in any creature has been imparted from the Creator, but God's goodness is underived, for it is the essence of His eternal nature. As God is infinite in power from all eternity, before there was any display thereof, or any act of omnipotency put forth; so He was eternally good before there was any communication of His bounty, or any creature to whom it might be imparted or exercised. Thus, the first manifestation of this Divine perfection was in giving being to all things...God has in Himself an infinite and inexhaustible treasure of all blessedness enough to fill all things.[2]

TOWARDS ALL CREATION

God is good to all his creation in that he providentially cares for it: "The eyes of all look expectantly to You, and You give them their food in due season. You open Your hand and satisfy the desire of every living thing" (Psa. 145:15-16). He is our Provider "who gives food to all flesh, for His mercy endures forever" (Psa. 136:25). Indeed, "the Lord is good to all, and His tender mercies are over all His works" (Psa. 145:9).

TOWARDS MAN

The Bible declares the goodness of God towards man: "Oh, how great is Your goodness, which You have laid up for those who fear You, which You have prepared for those who trust in You in the presence of the sons of men!" (Psa. 31:19). Please note that God's goodness is laid up for those who fear and trust God. "The Lord is good, a stronghold in the day of trouble; and He knows those who trust in Him" (Nah. 1:7). Those who seek God will enjoy the "good things" of God:

> Ask, and it will be given to you; seek, and you will find; knock, and it will be opened to you. For everyone who asks receives, and he who seeks finds, and to him who knocks it will be opened. Or what man is there among you who, if his son asks for bread, will give him a stone? Or if he asks for a fish, will he give him a serpent? If you then, being evil, know how to give good gifts to your children, how much more will your Father who is in heaven give good things to those who ask Him! (Matt. 7:7-11)

The goodness of God towards man has its greatest manifestation in the sending of his Son to die for sinful man to purchase their redemption.

God has indeed been so good toward man when he least deserved it. Yet many turn away in their ignorance and stubborn will from God and his rich blessings. Why would men "despise the riches of His goodness, forbearance, and longsuffering, not knowing that the goodness of God leads you to repentance" (Rom. 2:4)? Everyone should stop and "consider the goodness and severity of God: on those who fell, severity; but toward you, goodness, if you continue in His goodness. Otherwise you also will be cut off" (Rom. 11:22). God's good blessings in Christ will continue with us IF we continue in his goodness.

It thrills the Christian's heart to contemplate the vast realm of the goodness of God. He was kind and loving to us when we were in sin, and he is incredibly good to us in Christ as one of his children. Even in our darkest hours, we must never be blinded by the sickness, pain, sorrow, or fears of a sinful world and fail to see the bright rays of God's goodness all around. "Oh, that men would give thanks to the Lord for His goodness, and for His wondrous works to the children of men! For He satisfies the longing soul, and fills the hungry soul with goodness" (Psa. 107:8-9).

THE COMPASSION OF GOD

Knowing that God is full of goodness, it is no surprise to learn that he is full of compassion. Our English word "compassion" means "pity for suffering, with desire to help or to spare; commiseration; sympathy."[3] The Greek word, *splanchnizomai*, means "to be moved as to one's inwards (*splanchna*), to be moved with compassion, to yearn with compassion."[4] It is to be moved with passion toward the plight of another, along with a strong desire to alleviate their suffering. Our Lord looks upon our lowly condition with compassion. It is a part of his nature.

GOD IS FULL OF COMPASSION

God is described as *full* of compassion (Psa. 86:15; 111:4; 112:4; 145:8). There were times of judgment, as with the nation of Israel, but God reserved compassion for the faithful who endured in their faith and hope (Lam. 3:31-32; Mic. 7:19).

Jesus demonstrated the compassionate heart of God while here on this earth. As he saw the great multitudes "he was moved with compassion for them, because they were like sheep not having a shepherd. So He began to teach them many things" (Mk. 6:34). As God looks upon the earth today, does he still not have compassion on those who are wandering about aimlessly as sheep without a shepherd? What is needed now is what he provided then – the teaching of truth that will guide the lost soul.

Jesus' compassion moved him to heal the sick, open the eyes of the blind, cleanse the lepers, and raised the dead (Matt. 14:14; 20:34; Mk. 1:41; Lk. 7:13). He also was compassionate to feed the hungry (Matt. 15:32). These examples of divine compassion show that God is quite willing to heal our spiritual sicknesses and feed our souls. The Lord is compassionate toward our physical infirmities (Heb. 4:15). Compassion is why God "delights" in mercy and pardoning our iniquities (Mic. 7:18-19).

WE ARE TO SHOW COMPASSION

Compassion is the reason that the master forgave the large debt of his servant in the parable of the unforgiving servant (Matt. 18:27). Yet, the servant turned around and refused to forgive the debt of a fellow servant. Why? That servant lacked compassion. As the master said, "Should you not also have had compassion on your fellow servant, just as I had pity on you?" (v. 33). The key to forgiveness is compassion. If we do not show compassion toward others, we will not teach them, help them, or forgive them. And such an attitude will not be welcomed in the eternal presence of a God who has shown such great compassion to us. Listen to the admonition of Scripture:

> Finally, all of you be of one mind, having compassion for one another; love as brothers, be tenderhearted, be courteous; not returning evil for evil or reviling for reviling, but on the contrary blessing, knowing that you were called to this, that you may inherit a blessing (1 Pet. 3:8-9).

THE FORGIVENESS OF GOD

A good and compassionate God is also one who is eager and willing to forgive the trespasses of men. "For You, Lord, are good, and ready to forgive, and abundant in mercy to all those who call upon You" (Psa. 86:5). On the one hand, we understand that God sees all our sins, but on the other hand we see that he is forgiving: "If You, Lord, should mark iniquities, O Lord, who could stand? But there is forgiveness with You, that You may be feared" (Psa. 130:3-4). What a comfort to the soul burdened with the guilt of sin! Without the promise of forgiveness, we would have no hope when facing the judgment of a holy and just God.

THE CONDITIONS OF GOD'S FORGIVENESS

If one desires to be forgiven by God, they must meet the conditions that God has given to obtain his forgiveness. The apostle Peter preached that sinners must "repent, and let every one of you be baptized in the name of

Jesus Christ for the remission of sins" (Acts 2:38), and "repent therefore and be converted, that your sins may be blotted out" (Acts 3:19). An alien sinner will be forgiven of their sins and become a Christian when he hears (Rom. 10:17), believes (Jn. 8:24), repents of sin (Acts 17:30), confesses Christ (Rom. 10:9-10), and is baptized in water (Acts 22:16).

When a child of God sins, he has the promise of God's forgiveness if he repents and confesses that sin. Simon the sorcerer was commanded to "repent therefore of this your wickedness, and pray God if perhaps the thought of your heart may be forgiven you" (Acts 8:22). The Scriptures promise that "if we confess our sins, He is faithful and just to forgive us our sins and to cleanse us from all unrighteousness" (1 Jn. 1:9). God's forgiveness is constantly available, but his conditions must be met.

OUR FORGIVENESS OF OTHERS

God's forgiveness of our sins depends greatly on our forgiveness of those who have sinned against us. Jesus taught us to pray, "And forgive us our debts, as we forgive our debtors" (Matt. 6:12), and then added, "For if you forgive men their trespasses, your heavenly Father will also forgive you. But if you do not forgive men their trespasses, neither will your Father forgive your trespasses" (vv. 14-15). Jesus warned that God will judge us severely "if each of you, from his heart, does not forgive his brother his trespasses" (Matt. 18:35). We are to "be kind to one another, tenderhearted, forgiving one another, just as God in Christ also forgave you" (Eph. 4:32). With that forgiveness comes a restoration of relationship; otherwise it is just words that have no meaning.

The condition for our forgiving another is the same as with God: *repentance*. We are to always be ready to forgive, just like God, but forgiveness itself is extended only when there is repentance expressed by the sinner. As Jesus taught, "If your brother sins against you, rebuke him; and if he repents, forgive him" (Lk. 17:3). Until one repents, they are living in sin and need the loving rebuke of faithful Christians. If he repents, we are commanded to forgive (cf. 2 Cor. 2:7-8).[5] Let us be ready to extend to others what God has so graciously extended to us – the forgiveness of sins.

THE IMMUTABILITY OF GOD

As we think about the wonderful and awesome characteristics of God, we learn that we can fully trust that God will always be what he is, that he will not change as to his eternal nature and character. This is what is meant by the immutability of God.

To say that God is immutable is to say that he does not change or cannot change…It has to do not only with God's essence but also – and perhaps even primarily – with his purposes and his works, especially his work of redemption. Its central core is *faithfulness*. That God is immutable means that he is faithful and true to his word; he does not waver in the carrying out of his promises.[6]

GOD DOES NOT CHANGE

After the Psalmist declares that the earth and the heavens will grow old and change, he declares, "But You are the same, and Your years will have no end" (Psa. 102:25-27). Here he affirms the immutability ("same") and eternity ("no end") of God. The classic text on God's immutability is Malachi 3:6 – "For I am the Lord, I do not change." The context emphasizes God's faithfulness to the covenant and love for Israel to keep them from utter destruction. This is quite a contrast from man's constant unfaithfulness. Unfaithful King Saul was told that "the Strength of Israel will not lie nor relent [change his mind]. For He is not a man, that He should relent" (1 Sam. 15:29).

God's faithfulness to his will and promises derive from the fact that he is unchangeable in his nature and character. The Father is described as one who provides every good and perfect gift for he is one "with whom there is no variation or shadow of turning" (Jas. 1:17). He can always be trusted to provide good things, because that is according to his unchangeable nature. This same principle is stated concerning Jesus Christ who is the "same yesterday, today, and forever" (Heb. 13:8). "He never needs to be replaced, and nothing can be added to his perfect work."[7]

WHEN GOD DOES CHANGE HIS MIND

There are instances in the Bible when God does "change" his mind. One famous example was concerning the destruction of Nineveh. Jonah warned Nineveh that they would be destroyed in forty days (Jonah 3:4). When the king and the people of Nineveh repented before God, it is said that "God saw their works, that they turned from their evil way; and God relented [changed his mind] from the disaster that He had said He would bring upon them, and He did not do it" (v. 10). This was a complete turn from the original plan, but *it was still consistent with the will and character of God*. Even Jonah admitted that God was "One who relents from doing harm" (4:2). When God's will involves conditions that a man or nation must meet, God will react one of two ways (destruction or forgiveness) depending on the actions of a man or nation (for a nation see Jer.18:7-10, and for an individual see Ezek. 18:20-28).

It is important to add that God's immutability does not mean that if a Christian sins and falls from grace (Gal. 5:4), God will not punish him. Indeed he will, for God provides both goodness *and* severity, depending on our actions.[8] And it also does not mean that God cannot change laws and covenants when he desires. This he did when Jesus brought the new covenant to man (Heb. 8).

GOD'S IMMUTABILITY AND THE CHRISTIAN

The Christian can establish his full *trust* in the immutable God. Knowing that you can fully trust all that God says and does to be true and just is "strong consolation" (Heb. 6:18). God cannot, and will not, lie to us (Tit. 1:2).

God's immutability also gives us *courage* and *peace of mind*. We will not stand before the judgment of God and find out we have been duped by some cosmic joke. When unbelieving men laugh and look down on us, we can be fully confident that God will reward his servants some day and put to shame those who do not believe. While others live nervously worrying whether men will keep their word, we live with the "peace of God, which surpasses all understanding" (Phil. 4:7).

Our *hope* is securely anchored in the immutable counsel of God himself. Our reservation in heaven is absolutely certain if we remain faithful to him (1 Pet. 1:3-5). The sinner, on the other hand, should tremble at the thought of the certain judgment of God. No excuses will help those who have refused the divine call of salvation.

God's goodness, compassion, and forgiveness are all part of God's immutable nature. Let us not despise his goodness and reject our opportunity to partake in the wonderful expressions of his good will toward men in Christ Jesus.

 QUESTIONS

1. Define "goodness." _____

_____

2. How can we know the standard of what is good? _____
_____

3. Where can we see God's first act of goodness? _____
_____

4. How is God continually good to his creation? _____
_____
_____

5. To whom will God give good things? _____
_____

6. What is the meaning of compassion? _____
_____
_____

7. Why did Jesus look upon the multitudes with compassion? _____
_____
_____

8. What is compassion the key to? _____
_____
_____

9. What does it mean that God is "ready to forgive"? _____
_____
_____

10. What are the conditions for a child of God to be forgiven? _____
_____
_____

11. What depends on our forgiving others? _____
_____
_____

12. What does "immutability" mean? _____
_____
_____

13. Name something about God that does not change. _____
_____
_____

14. Describe the three blessings the Christian finds in the immutable God.
   a. _____
   _____
   b. _____
   _____
   c. _____
   _____

FILL IN THE BLANK AND GIVE THE SCRIPTURE

1. "...the earth is full of the _____ of the Lord" (_____)

2. "The Lord is _____ to all, and His _____ mercies are over all His works" (_____)

3. "Oh, that men would give _____ to the Lord for His _____...For He satisfies the _____ soul, and fills the _____ soul with _____" (_____)

4. "Finally, all of you be of one mind, having _____ for one an- other..." (_____)

5. ...O Lord, who could _____? But there is _____ with You..." (_____)

6. "But you are the _____, and Your years will have no _____" (_____)

TRUE OR FALSE

1. _____ The goodness of God can help us even in our darkest hours.
2. _____ God is described as "full" of compassion.
3. _____ God's compassion will save everyone regardless of how they have lived.
4. _____ We should forgive others even if they have not repented.
5. _____ Since God does not change, once I'm saved, I'm always saved.

6. _____ I can fully trust that the Bible is true and that God will keep his promises.

THOUGHT QUESTIONS

1. How do we answer someone who argues that since God is so loving, good, and compassionate, he will somehow save everyone?

2. How would you explain the phrase "God is faithful" (1 Cor. 1:9; 10:13) in view of the immutability of God?

GOD'S FIERCE
WRATH

Most enjoy thinking about the wonderful blessings the love of God provides. However, many do not want to meditate on God's fierce wrath and the pain and suffering he is capable of inflicting on them. God wants us to be aware of his immeasurable love and his awesome wrath. "Therefore consider the goodness and severity of God; on those who fell, severity; but towards you, goodness, if you continue in His goodness. Otherwise you also will be cut off" (Rom. 11:22).

"The Bible has a voice of warning and denunciation, as well as words of invitation and love. Whoever omits the warning of the judgment, speaks but half the message which God would have him deliver. God's wrath is his resentment against sin...."[1] In years past, some preachers were described as "hell fire and brimstone preachers." This description is seldom heard today for many preachers neglect to preach about God's terrible wrath. They fear it will make those listening uncomfortable. Therefore, many are not afraid of disobeying God because they have "no fear of God" (Rom. 3:18). Most are not afraid to speak God's name in vain (Ex. 20:7)!

"FIERCENESS OF HIS WRATH"

God warned the Israelites that if they "afflict any widows or fatherless child...My wrath will become hot, and I will kill you with the sword; your wives will be widows, and your children fatherless" (Ex. 22:22-24). When Israel worshiped the golden calf that Aaron made, God said to Moses, "Now therefore, let Me alone, that My wrath may burn hot against them and I may consume them" (Ex. 32:1-10). Moses pleaded with God, "Turn from Your fierce wrath and relent from this harm to Your people" (Ex. 32:12). God listened to Moses' plea for mercy for Israel.

In Revelation, one reads about "the fierceness of His wrath" (16:19) and "the fierceness and wrath of Almighty God" (19:15). We must serve God "with reverence and godly fear. For our God is a consuming fire" (Heb. 12:28, 29). "It is a fearful thing to fall into the hands of the living God" (Heb. 10:21).

GOD'S FIERCE WRATH IS JUST

The Divine wrath is to be regarded as the natural expression of the Divine nature, which is absolute holiness, manifesting itself against the willful high-handed, deliberate, inexcusable sin and iniquity of mankind. God's wrath is always regarded in the Scripture as the just, proper, and natural expression of His holiness and righteousness which must always, under all circumstances, and all costs be maintained. It is therefore a righteous indignation and compatible with the holy and righteous nature of God....[2]

If he was not wrathful and warring against sin, God would then, in effect, be saying that sinfulness is not evil and can be tolerated. That would be a lie, because sinfulness is evil. But God cannot lie and be untrue to his essential Being, which is holy and loving. If God were to tolerate sin in not having a sustained wrath against it, it would mean he accepted sinfulness as a legitimate assault on his holiness (because God is holy) and that he finds human suffering caused by evil to be acceptable. But God is supremely holy and just – and he is pure Love. Thus, his nature and Being cannot tolerate sinfulness and that which violates who and what he is. Therefore, it is impossible for a just God not to have "wrath" toward sin.[3]

This wrath is related to the love of God, as Pukiser points out. "Nor is there a contradiction between God's wrath and His love. Wrath is the other side, the obverse, of love. Since God is love, He cannot tolerate that which destroys those He loves, wrecks havoc in His universe, and tramples underfoot His holy will. Wrath is the unfailing opposition of God's holy love to all that is evil.[4]

GOD'S CHASTENING IS PROOF OF HIS LOVE FOR US

"My son, do not despise the chastening of the Lord, nor detest His correction; for whom the Lord loves He corrects just as the father the son in whom he delights" (Prov. 3:11-12; Heb. 12:5-6). God knows that sin will destroy our happiness both now and eternally (Rom. 6:23; Jas. 1:15).

There are many verses in Proverbs that tell of the horrible consequences of a sinful life (1:10-19, 24-33; 2:10-22; 4:14-17; 5:1-14).

PROPER DISCIPLINE OF CHILDREN SHOWS LOVE
Parents, who love their children, will punish them for bad behavior and attitudes (Prov. 13:24; 23:13-14; 29:15). They know that bad behavior and attitudes will cause their children much grief both now and eternally. My parents often said to me, before punishing me, "This hurts me more than it does you." Now, that I am a parent, I know it is true. It is indifference, not love, which causes parents to overlook their children's ungodly behavior and attitudes.

GOD IS "SLOW TO ANGER"
How thankful we should be that our wonderful heavenly Father is "slow to anger" (Neh. 9:17; Psa. 103:8; 145:8)! The prophets often mention God's reluctance to punish those whom he created. "So rend your heart, and not your garments; return to the Lord your God, for He is gracious and merciful, slow to anger, and of great kindness; and He relents from doing harm" (Joel 2:13).[5] Jonah was very angry with God because he did not destroy the people of Nineveh when they repented of their evil ways (Jonah 3-4). Micah tells us why God wants to pardon our sins: "He does not retain His anger forever, for He delights in mercy" (7:18-19).

WE MUST BE "SLOW TO WRATH"
God wants his children to be "slow to wrath" like him. "Therefore, my beloved brethren, let every man be swift to hear, slow to speak, slow to wrath; for the wrath of man does not produce the righteousness of God" (Jas. 1:19-20). Those "slow to wrath": have "great understanding" (Prov. 14:29); will appease strife (Prov. 15:18); and are "better than the mighty" (Prov. 16:32).

JESUS POSSESSES ANGER
Jesus became very angry when he found some desecrating the holy temple. They were selling oxen, sheep, and doves on the grounds of the temple. He "made a whip of cords, He drove them all out of the temple" and vehemently demanded "Take these things away! Do not make My Father's house a house of merchandise" (Jn. 2:13-17)!

The Pharisees watched Jesus intently to see if he would heal a man with a withered hand on the Sabbath. If he did, they would accuse him of breaking the Sabbath. Jesus said, "'Is it lawful on the Sabbath to do good or to do evil, to save life or to kill?' But they kept silent. So when He had looked around with anger, being grieved by the hardness of their hearts..." (Mk. 3:1-5). His anger was a righteous indignation caused by a calloused attitude toward him.

RIGHTEOUS INDIGNATION

Indignation means, "anger or scorn resulting from injustice, ingratitude, or meanness; righteous anger." "Anger at the sin and unrighteousness of men, and because their sin is grievous to God, may be called a 'righteous indignation'...Anger, while likely to become sinful, is not really sinful in itself."[7] Paul wrote by inspiration, "'Be angry and do not sin'; do not let the sun go down on your wrath, nor give place to the devil" (Eph. 4:26-27).

GOD HATES SIN!

The Father said to his Son, "You have loved righteousness and hated lawlessness" (Heb. 1:8, 9). David wrote, "For You *are* not a God who takes pleasure in wickedness, nor shall evil dwell with You. The boastful shall not stand in Your sight; you hate all workers of iniquity. You shall destroy those who speak falsehood; The Lord abhors the bloodthirsty and deceitful man" (Psa. 5:4-6).

WE MUST HATE SIN

God wants us to hate those things that he hates. Those "who love the Lord, hate evil" (Psa. 97:10). We should hate sin because it deeply grieves God (Gen. 6:5, 6) and it severs our fellowship with our holy Father (Isa. 59:1-2). Solomon wrote in Proverbs, "The fear of the Lord is to hate evil; pride and arrogance and the evil way and the perverse mouth I hate" (8:13); "A righteous man hates lying" (13:5); and, "...he who hates covetousness will prolong his days" (28:16).[8] The Psalmist said, "I hate every false way" (119:104, 128). In the New Testament, we are commanded, "Abhor what is evil. Cling to what is good" (Rom. 12:9).

The reason we are often guilty of sin is that we have failed to cultivate a hatred for evil. We often seek the "pleasure in unrighteousness" (2 Thess. 2:12). Do we possess righteous indignation toward everything that would destroy our fellowship with God?

EXAMPLES OF GOD'S FIERCE WRATH IN THE OLD TESTAMENT

GOD FLOODS THE EARTH

The enormous wickedness of man grieved God so much that he "was sorry that He had made man on the earth, and He was grieved in His heart. So the Lord said, 'I will destroy man whom I have created from the face of the earth, both man and beast, creeping things and birds of the air, for I am sorry that I have made them'" (Gen. 6:5-7). Because "Noah found favor in the eyes of the Lord" (Gen. 6:8), the Lord told him to build an ark (vv. 13-21). Noah built the ark "according to all that God commanded him" (v. 22). Only eight people boarded the ark and were saved from the flood (1 Pet. 3:20). As the flood waters rose, many people must have desperately begged to be allowed in the ark. Soon their pitiful cries ended for they had drowned. Can you imagine how horrible they must have felt as the water rose higher and higher and they realized they would drown?

"The Lord Rained Brimstone and Fire"
The inhabitants of Sodom and Gomorrah were very wicked. They were guilty of practicing homosexuality (Gen. 19:4-11). God hates this sexual perversion (Lev. 18:22; 20:13; Rom. 1:26-27)! Because of their "very grievous" sin (Gen. 18:20), "the Lord rained brimstone and fire on Sodom and Gomorrah...God destroyed the cities of the plain" (Gen. 19:24-29). Their fiery death should serve as an example to all "who live ungodly" (2 Pet. 2:6; Jude 7). Can you imagine the terrifying scene of fire falling on people and hearing their agonizing screams as they burned to death?

Egypt and Israel felt "the Fierceness of His Anger"
God brought ten awful plagues upon the Egyptians which included the death of their firstborn (Ex. 5-11). The Israelites saw the devastation and misery those plagues caused the Egyptians. However, they failed miserably to be terrified of incurring God's wrath.

In the wilderness, they provoked the Lord's anger by doubting his ability to provide water and food for them (Psa. 78:17-20). "Therefore the LORD heard *this* and was furious; so a fire was kindled against Jacob, and anger also came up against Israel, because they did not believe in God, and did not trust in His salvation" (Psa. 78:21-22). Because they insisted on worshiping idols, which God had emphatically forbidden, "he was furious, and greatly abhorred Israel" (Psa. 78:56-59). He severely punished them by delivering them "...into captivity, and His glory into the enemy's hand. He also gave His people over to the sword, and was furious with His inheritance. The fire consumed their young men, and their maidens were not given in marriage. Their priests fell by the sword, and their widows made no lamentation" (Psa. 78:60-64). Are you afraid of disobeying the Almighty One?

EXAMPLES OF GOD'S FIERCE WRATH IN THE NEW TESTAMENT

GOD KILLED ANANIAS AND SAPPHIRA

This husband and wife sold some land and "brought a certain part and laid it at the apostles' feet" (Acts 5:1-2). They must have pretended to be giving all the money from the sale of their property for Peter said, "You have not lied to men but to God" (vv. 3-4). Ananias "fell down and breathed his last" (v. 5). Because Sapphira also lied "she fell down at his feet and breathed her last" (vv. 6-10). "So great fear came upon all the church and upon all who heard these things" (v. 11). Does this example of God's fierce wrath toward lying cause you to be afraid of lying? It should for "all liars shall have their part in the lake which burns with fire and brimstone" (Rev. 21:8).

"An Angel of the Lord Struck" Herod
Herod Agrippa I "gave an oration...And the people kept shouting, 'The voice of a god and not of a man!' Then immediately an angel of the Lord struck him, because he did not give glory to God. And he was eaten by worms and died" (Acts 12:20-23). "Josephus...says that Herod was seized with violent pains in the bowels, and that he lingered in great torture for five days."[9] "God resists the proud" for the proud resist him and do not seek him (Jas. 4:6; Psa. 10:4). Does this example of God's fierce wrath toward pride cause you to be afraid of being puffed up with pride (Prov. 16:18)? A wise person will learn from the mistakes of others.

"FEAR GOD" (1 PETER 2:17)

The Greek words, which are translated "fear," have several meanings. W. E. Vine, defines the Greek word *phobos*, "(a) fear, dread, terror... (b) reverential fear, (1) of God, as a controlling motive of life, in matters spiritual and moral, not a fear of His power and righteous retribution, but a wholesome dread of displeasing Him, a fear which banishes the terror that shrinks from His presence...."[10]

The fear, which "perfect love casts out," is the fear of want, death, and the terror of judgment (1 Jn. 4:18; Matt. 10:28; Heb. 13:6). This is a fear that comes from disobedient living and lack of faith in the wonderful attributes of God. True love for God casts out such fear because one believes wholeheartedly in the goodness and faithfulness of God to keep his promises (Tit. 1:2; Heb. 10:23).

FAILURE TO FEAR GOD RESULTS IN EVIL LIVES

Living a wicked, immoral, godless life is the disastrous result of a failure to fear God. "An oracle within my heart concerning the transgression of the wicked: There is no fear of God before his eyes. For he flatters himself in his own eyes, when he finds out his iniquity and when he hates. The words of his mouth are wickedness and deceit; he has ceased to be wise and to do good. He devises wickedness on his bed; he sets himself in a way that is not good; he does not abhor evil" (Psa. 36:1-4). The Lord asked the Hebrews, whom he considered "a special treasure to Me above all people" (Ex. 19:5), "'Do you not fear Me?' says the Lord. 'Will you not tremble at My presence...?' ...But this people has a defiant and rebellious heart; they have revolted and departed. They do not say in their heart, 'Let us now fear the Lord our God, who gives rain both the former and the latter, in its season. He reserves for us the appointed weeks of the harvest.' Your iniquities have turned these things away, and your sins have withheld good things from you" (Jer. 5:20-25). Both Jews and Greeks "were all under sin" (Rom. 3:9). "There is none righteous, no, not one..." (Rom. 3:10-17). The cause for their being completely submerged in ungodliness was "There is no fear of God before their eyes" (Rom. 3:18).

THE BLESSINGS FOR FEARING GOD

"Praise the Lord! Blessed is the man who fears the Lord, who delights greatly in His commandments" (Psa. 112:1). "He has given food to those who fear Him" (Psa. 111:5). "He will fulfill the desire of those who fear Him; He also will hear their cry and save them. The Lord preserves all who love Him, but all the wicked He will destroy" (Psa. 145:19-20). "The fear of the Lord is clean" (Psa. 19:9). Job said, "And to man He said, 'Behold, the fear of the Lord, that is wisdom, and to depart from evil is understanding'" (Job 28:28). If you will allow the teaching of God's word to mold your character and guide your life, you will live a clean, pure, wholesome life.

"The fear of the Lord is the beginning of wisdom; a good understanding have all those who do His commandments" (Psa. 111:10). Meditating on God's word will give you such valuable knowledge that you will: be wiser than your enemies; have more understanding than your teachers; and "understand more than the ancients" (Psa. 119:98-100; Prov. 1:7). The knowledge and wisdom found in the Bible is more valuable than gold (Psa. 19:10-11)! Does your life prove that you believe the Bible is more valuable than gold?

If you will be filled "with reverence and godly fear": you will be accepted by God (Acts 10:34-35); your service to God will please him (Heb. 12:28); and "it will be well" with your soul (Eccl. 8:12). "But it will not be well with the wicked; nor will he prolong his days which are as a shadow, because he does not fear before God" (Eccl. 8:13).

"Conclusion of the Whole Matter" (Ecclesiastes 12:13)

Solomon concluded that "the whole duty of man" is to "fear God and keep His commandments" (Eccl. 12:13). Knowing that God will judge your works "without partiality," you should "conduct yourselves throughout the time of your sojourning here in fear" (1 Pet. 1:17).

Unforgiven Sinners will Feel God's Wrath

"For the wrath of God is revealed from heaven against ungodliness and unrighteousness of men, who suppress the truth in unrighteousness" (Rom. 1:18). If you have a hard and "impenitent heart you are treasuring up for yourself wrath in the day of wrath and revelation of the righteous judgment of God, who 'will render to each one according to his deeds': eternal life to those who by patient continuance in doing good seek for glory, honor, and immortality; but to those who are self-seeking and do not obey the truth, but obey unrighteousness—indignation and wrath, tribulation and anguish, on every soul of man who does evil, of the Jew first and also of the Greek; but glory, honor, and peace to everyone who works what is good, to the Jew first and also to the Greek" (Rom. 2:5-10).

Salvation from God's Wrath

The good, merciful, gracious, loving heavenly Father has provided a means of salvation from his fierce wrath through the blood of his Son. "But God demonstrates His own love toward us, in that while we were still sinners, Christ died for us. Much more then, having now been justified by His blood, we shall be saved from wrath through Him. For if when we were enemies we were reconciled to God through the death of His Son, much more, having been reconciled, we shall be saved by His life" (Rom. 5:8-10). The blood of Jesus will wash "us from our sins" (Rev. 1:5) when we are baptized into his death where his precious blood was shed (Acts 22:16: Rom. 6:3; Jn. 19:34). Why would anyone refuse to comply with God's gracious plan to save one from his wrath?

✎ Questions ✎

Fill in the Blank (give scripture where required)

1. God wants us to be aware of his immeasurable _____ and awesome _____.

2. "Therefore consider the _____ and _____ of God." (_____)

3. Many are not afraid of God's _____ because they have "no _____ of _____."

4. _____ pleaded with God to turn from his fierce _____.

5. In _____, one reads about "the _____ of His _____." (_____)

6. We must serve God with _____ and _____ _____.

7. God's fierce _____ is _____.

8. It is impossible for a _____ God not to have _____ toward _____.

9. _____ has many verses describing the horrible consequences of a _____ life.

10. It is _____, not _____ that causes parents to overlook their _____ bad behavior.

11. "So rend your _____, and not your _____." (_____)

12. Those "slow to wrath": have great _____; will appease _____; and are better than the _____.

13. "Do not make My Father's _____ a _____ of _____!" (_____)

14. "You _____ all workers of _____." (_____)

15. We often sin because we seek the "_____ in _____."

TRUE OR FALSE

1. ___ God threatened to destroy the Israelites.
2. ___ God delights in punishing sinners.
3. ___ God delights in showing mercy.
4. ___ It is possible to be angry and not sin.
5. ___ One may love the Lord and not hate evil.

6. ___ After God closed the door of the ark, ten people got aboard.
7. ___ The Israelites often provoked God to anger in the wilderness.
8. ___ God killed Ananias and Sapphira because of their pride.
9. ___ Herod died from a heart attack.
10. __ A foolish person learns from the mistakes of others.

MATCH THE VERSE WITH THE CORRECT SCRIPTURE REFERENCE

1. ___ "For our God is a consuming fire"   a. Genesis 6:8
2. ___ "You have loved righteousness & hated lawlessness"   b. Psa. 36:1
3. ___ "A righteous man hates lying"   c. Romans 2:5
4. ___ "Noah found favor in the eyes of the Lord"   d. Genesis 19:24
5. ___ "Then the Lord rained brimstone and fire..."   e. Ecclesiastes 8:13
6. ___ "Therefore the Lord heard this and was furious"   f. Hebrews 12:29
7. ___ "There is no fear of God before his eyes"   g. Proverbs 13:5
8. ___ "Do you not fear Me?"   h. Romans 5:9
9. ___ "Blessed is the man who fears the Lord"   i. Hebrews 1:9
10. ___ "...it will be well with those who fear God"   j. Jeremiah 5:22
11. ___ "But it will not be well with the wicked"   k. Ecclesiastes 12:13
12. ___ "Fear God and keep His commandments"   l. Psalm 78:21
13. ___ "...you are treasuring up for yourself wrath..."   m. Psalm 112:1
14. ___ "...we shall be saved from wrath through Him"   n. Acts 22:16
15. ___ "Arise and be baptized and wash away your sins"   o. Eccl. 8:12

THOUGHT QUESTIONS

1. How does proper discipline of children show love?

2. Define and give an example of righteous indignation.

3. How did Jesus make it possible for us to escape God's fierce wrath?

THE PROVIDENCE OF GOD

The providence of God is both a fascinating and challenging subject to consider. It deals generally with the sovereign control and activity of God in the physical and spiritual realms. It can be quite difficult to recognize because it is non-miraculous and "behind the scenes." David recognized God's providential activity and its affect on the course of human events when he said to Abigail, "Blessed be the Lord God of Israel, who sent you this day to meet me!" (1 Sam. 25:32). The Lord had not commanded Abigail to go and calm David's anger, but her good character put her in a position to fulfill God's will. A careful study of the providence of God will increase our faith and trust in his perfect ability to work his plan and purpose for man's eternal salvation.

WHAT IS "PROVIDENCE"?

"Providence" comes from the concept "to provide." These words derive from the Latin words *providentia* and *providere* meaning "to foresee, foresight, forethought."[1] The Greek word *pronoia* means "forethought... is translated 'providence' in Acts 24:2; 'provision' in Rom. 13:14."[2]

Though Acts 24:2 deals with the providence of men, the term is mainly used today about the actions of God. The concept involves divine foresight, care, guardianship, supervision, and control through natural means toward a future goal. Note the following definitions of the providence of God:

> ...the working of God through His provision in the natural and spiritual realms; it is a working control in both which neither violates the sovereignty of the human will nor the divine natural and spiritual laws...Divine providence is a distinctive feature or attribute

whereby the omniscience and omnipotence of the infinite God finds expression.[3]

> The providence of God concerns itself with the preservation, care, and government which God exercises over everything that He has created, in order that they may accomplish the purpose for which they were created.[4]
>
> ...God is not only active in the world, but is active in *all* the world, in *everything* that happens (though not necessarily in the same way): the known and the unknown, the familiar and the mysterious, the trivial and the spectacular, the minute and the majestic, the sad and the joyful, the painful and the pleasant, the good and the evil. For this is the idea of providence: not that God is merely "on call" and *ready* to act if needed, nor that he is active only in the sunshine and not in the shadow, but that he is indeed a "God who acts" – always and everywhere.[5]

God's providence has been described as "the hand of God in the glove of history." When we pray "Your will be done" (Matt. 6:10; Jas. 4:15), we should understand that our great and powerful God will make every provision for our needs, and is able to hear and answer our prayers as he works his divine purpose through the nations and individuals of human history.

GENERAL AND SPECIAL PROVIDENCE

General Providence refers to the care and supervision of God over the created universe. "All things were created through [Christ] and for Him. And He is before all things, and in Him all things consist" (Col. 1:16-17). God provides for the natural creation by sending water for the growth of vegetation and to give drink to the animals (Psa. 104:10-14). He also provides the sun and moon, light and darkness for the cycles of life to exist (vv. 19-23). We can observe this and declare, "O Lord, how manifold are Your works!" (v. 24). The Lord's sovereign rule over this earth means that "whatever the Lord pleases He does" (Psa. 135:5-7), and He keeps our world in perfect order.[6] The apostle Paul proclaimed God's providential care of our natural world to the idolatrous peoples of his day (Acts 14:17).

God's general providential care of the animal world is affirmed in Scripture (Psa. 104:11-18; 147:8-9). Jesus spoke of the Father's care of the animals: "Look at the birds of the air, for they neither sow nor reap nor gather into barns; yet your heavenly Father feeds them. Are you not of more value than they?" (Matt. 6:26; cf. 10:29).

God's providence also extends to the affairs of men in general. Job remarked, "He makes nations great, and destroys them; He enlarges nations, and guides them" (Job 12:23). Daniel adds, "And He changes the times and the seasons; He removes kings and raises up kings..." (Dan. 2:21; 4:25, 35). God extends His physical blessings to all men, "for He makes His sun rise on the evil and on the good, and sends rain on the just and on the unjust" (Matt. 5:45).

Special Providence refers to the specific care of God on behalf of those who are his people. God's people are to cast all their cares on God, for they have the promise that "He cares for you" (1 Pet. 5:7). This is the special care and concern of the heavenly Father for his spiritual children. He provides for his children the proper pathway of life: "The steps of a good man are ordered by the Lord, and He delights in his way. Though he fall, he shall not be utterly cast down; for the Lord upholds him with His hand" (Psa. 37:23-24; Prov. 3:5-6).

God will also help his children properly order their priorities and goals. He teaches us to "seek first the kingdom of God and His righteousness" (Matt. 6:33). God's righteous way will always work spiritual good for those who follow it: "And we know that all things work together for good to those who love God, to those who are the called according to His purpose" (Rom. 8:28).[7] Christians who obey God's word enjoy the blessed guidance of God, for "His divine power has given to us all things that pertain to life and godliness, through the knowledge of Him who called us by glory and virtue" (2 Pet. 1:3).

BIBLE EXAMPLES OF THE PROVIDENCE OF GOD

JOSEPH

Joseph could have asked himself, "Why me?" or "Why now?" on many occasions in his life. God worked "behind the scenes" over many years to place Joseph in Egypt at a precise time that would affect all of Bible history afterward (Gen. 37-50). God had a grand plan in mind, but Joseph did not fully recognize his place in that plan until after he had endured many unusual and difficult situations. Notice his words to his brothers after he revealed himself to them in Egypt:

> I am Joseph your brother, who you sold into Egypt. But now, do not therefore be grieved or angry with yourselves because you

sold me here; for God sent me before you to preserve life…So now it was not you who sent me here, but God; and He has made me a father to Pharaoh, and lord of all his house, and a ruler throughout all the land of Egypt (Gen. 45:4-5, 8; cf. 50:19-20).

Joseph understood that it was God who had orchestrated the events that put him in such a unique position. Joseph is describing the providential work of God. Hindsight and historical analysis can help us recognize the divine purpose working in history, even as it works through tragic and sad events. God is able to influence events of history and use the choices of men to advance his ultimate purpose. As for Joseph, he remained faithful and trusting in God throughout all the events of his life, and God worked through him and his righteous choices to advance his will (cf. Job 1:8).

ESTHER

Esther, and her cousin, Mordecai, were among the Jews that had been scattered by the Babylonian captivity, and they chose to remain in the kingdom of Persia where they had settled. Esther found herself chosen to be the queen of Ahasuerus, and was in this unique position when evil Haman conspired to destroy the Jews (Esther 1-3). Mordecai recognized that Esther was in "the right place at the right time," and wanted her to make supplication to the king on behalf of her people (4:6-9). Esther responded that she did not have permission to have an audience with the king, and to call upon him would mean death (4:10-12). Mordecai's words to her reveal his belief in the providence of God:

Do not think in your heart that you will escape in the king's palace any more than all the other Jews. For if you remain completely silent at this time, relief and deliverance will arise for the Jews from another place, but you and your father's house will perish. Yet who knows whether you have come to the kingdom for such a time as this? (Esther 4:13-14).

Mordecai understood that we must act faithfully in order to help fulfill the will of God. God will always fulfill his purpose in this world, but we cannot be certain how he may use us in doing this. We must continue to work what is good so that we can be in "the right place at the right time," even to face a tragedy with godly endurance and faith. Thankfully, Esther was persuaded to do what was right regardless of the consequences, saying, "if I perish, I perish!" (4:16). God was able to use faithful Esther to save the entire nation of Jews (Esther 5-10). God is never mentioned by name in the book of Esther, but we clearly see him there through his providence.

IMPORTANT PRINCIPLES ABOUT
GOD, MAN, AND DIVINE PROVIDENCE

There are important principles to keep in mind that will help guide our study of God's providence. These principles will keep our thinking within spiritual guidelines, and avoid unrestrained speculations and unlearned opinions.

First, *man in this natural realm is subject to all natural laws and consequences.* Life produces a variety of events in our life that will result in enjoyment and fulfillment (Eccl. 5:18-20), or accident, suffering, and death (Lk. 13:1-5). God allows both good and evil to exist in this world, and our daily choices will determine whether the good or evil has the greater affect on our lives. Choosing good companions will result in good benefits. Bad companionship will have a corrupting influence (1 Cor. 15:33). If you choose to step off a cliff, the natural law of gravity will produce negative consequences. On the other hand, if I determine to obey the laws of the land, the dangers of unrestrained living are dramatically reduced. The natural world was created and is upheld by the wisdom of God, and the more we respect and live according to God's physical laws, the better our mind, health, and attitude will be. It is the same principle in our spiritual lives. If one person walks according to the Spirit, and another is involved in the works of the flesh, there will be dramatically different lifestyles and consequences (Gal. 5:16-26)!

Second, *God is able to influence free moral beings without interfering with their free choice.* God can persuade, guide, influence, or hinder both individuals and nations without violating their free moral agency (1 Sam. 25:32-33; Hab. 1:5-6). God may even use the events of life to test the genuineness of our faith (Gen. 22:1; 1 Pet. 1:6-7; Jas. 1:2-3). We have free choice, but making our choices according to what would please God will put us in better position to be of use to God for his grand purposes. In the end, we are always responsible for our own choices and their consequences however God may use them to advance his will.

Third, *God can, and will, act according to his will in answer to the prayer of the faithful.* Prayer is an act of faith. We ask and receive in faith according to the will of God (Jas. 1:5-6). The Scripture says that the "effective, fervent, prayer of a righteous man avails much" (Jas. 5:16), but it remains with God alone as to what it avails, whether the answer is "yes" or "no," when, where, how, how much, etc. We must never dictate to God how or when he will answer our prayers, and we must be willing to accept his answer no matter what it is, or whether we like it or not. We know that God hears; we must trust him to answer in his time and in his way.[8]

Fourth, *providence deals ultimately with the spiritual goals of God's eternal purpose.* God's overall desire and purpose is that he might be glorified, and man participates in this by fearing and obeying God (1 Tim. 2:4; Eccl. 12:13). Any joy, pleasure, trial, suffering, or chastening that we endure in this life should lead to greater faith, endurance, and service to the glory of God. If we are faithful to God, we will fulfill our "whole duty" to fear him and keep his commandments in this life. If we are not faithful to God, we have no promise or hope in this life or the life to come.

False Ideas about the Providence of God

Unfortunately, false ideas have arisen and become quite popular in the thinking of many today, even Christians who should know better. The principles just discussed will help prevent many false ideas, but some still persist and must be answered.

First, some have the false idea that *everything that happens is totally predestined and controlled by God.* In other words, we are but "puppets" in a grand "play" completely controlled by God. This wrong thinking arises from a misunderstanding of the concepts of sovereignty, foreknowledge, predestination, and free will. The truth is that God allows both good and evil to exist in this world, and, consequently, the free will choices of men will have joyous or tragic consequences depending on those choices. Tragic events are not to be blamed on God, but on the evil choices that are made by man. Evil choices and events are not according to God's will, and Satan and his evil temptations should be blamed. God does not interfere with the free choices of men that often cause grief and suffering to those who are innocent and good. The righteous know that all accounts will be settled by the just and perfect judgment of God at the final day.

Second, some think that *if a tragedy happens to someone, it is because God is punishing them.* This was the position of the three friends of Job, who tried to convince Job that he was suffering because he was a sinner (Job 4:7-8; 11:6). God later told them that they had not spoken correctly (Job 42:7-8). Jesus also rejected this false idea by explaining that specific tragedies do **not** occur because some are "worse sinners" than others (Lk. 13:1-5). Evil, tragic events can happen to good people or bad people without partiality. One simply cannot take a particular tragic event and absolutely conclude that God meant it as a punishment.[9] Of course, good lessons can be learned in the aftermath of a tragedy, reminding young and old that there is no lasting hope in this life alone.[10]

Third, someone may say, *"Look how bad my life is – God doesn't love, help, or watch out for me!"* Some are quick to hold God responsible for every bad choice and event in their life. Again, we are responsible for our own choices, not God, who is no respecter of persons. There should be no question that God loves all men. He sent his Son to save mankind (Jn. 3:16) and invites all men to come to him (Matt. 11:28). A bad life can be made good again if we will "seek first the kingdom of God and His righteousness" (Matt. 6:33). A proper spiritual path and outlook will vastly improve our lives and attitude. It will not guarantee that problems and troubles will not still come our way, but we will be able to deal with them in a righteous, godly way. God can help us use trial and afflictions to strengthen ourselves spiritually (2 Cor. 12:7-10).

Fourth, someone may suggest that *it is useless to pray for health, safety, etc., because tragedies do, and will, occur.* Again, prayer is an act of faith and is to be offered according to God's will, not as a demand sheet for God to do or else! The fact is, God will not, and should not be expected to miraculously interfere with man's freedom to do foolish or evil things that cause accidents, disease, wars, and other tragedies that bring suffering to innocent people who are "in the wrong place at the wrong time."[11] In our unpredictable world, what should happen, or that we hope would happen, does not always happen:

> I returned and saw under the sun that – the race is not to the swift, nor the battle to the strong, nor bread to the wise, nor riches to men of understanding, nor favor to men of skill; but time and chance happen to them all. For man does not know his time: like fish taken in a cruel net, like birds caught in a snare, so the sons of men are snared in an evil time, when it falls suddenly upon them (Eccl. 9:11-12).

We must understand that a prayerful life will focus our minds and bodies to live godly and make righteous choices that will protect and spare our lives and the lives of our loved ones. The promise given to children who honor their parents, "that it may be well with you and you may live long on the earth" (Deut. 5:16; Eph. 6:2-3), is not an empty promise. Children who learn to respect and honor parental authority will lead lives that will keep them from evil choices and environments. A life filled with prayer, godly living, and righteous choices will help protect one from ungodly friends, intoxicants and drugs, living in the sexual "fast lane," taking foolish risks, and going to dangerous places. God's word is the key: "Your word I have hidden in my heart, that I may not sin against You" (Psa. 119:11). If we seek wisdom, she will preserve our way (Prov. 1:33 – 2:9).

God will not miraculously blow a tornado off course, keep a wheel from coming off a car, push a drunk driver away from a potential head-on collision, redirect a bullet from causing a mortal wound, prevent a molester from grabbing a child, or defuse a suicide bomber, but God can work in other ways we may not realize to help us and our loved ones avoid such dangers. *But even if tragedy does occur*, our faith in God's love, care, and sovereign rule must not waver! There must be no doubt that through God's love and care, we are spiritually safe in the arms of Jesus regardless of what happens in this world of sin and sorrow (Job 1:20-22). Even as we endure the "bad" things of life, our lives must be expressions of love and praise to the glory of God.

THE CHRISTIAN'S RESPONSE TO THE PROVIDENCE OF GOD

A better understanding of God's providence encourages positive responses in the faithful and trusting Christian.

The Christian is filled with *adoration and reverence* as he sees the wonderful and generous provisions of God in his everyday life. "Bless the Lord, O my soul, and forget not all His benefits" (Psa. 103:2). We would do well to often "stand still and consider the wondrous works of God" (Job 37:14).

The Christian will exhibit *humility* as he goes about his daily business. "Come now, you who say, 'Today or tomorrow we will go to such and such a city, spend a year there, buy and sell, and make a profit'; whereas you do not know what will happen tomorrow…Instead you ought to say, 'If the Lord wills, we shall live and do this and that'" (Jas. 4:13-15). Our lives are not our own to do as we wish, but are to be given to God's purposes, and to make our choices according to his will.

The Christian finds *freedom from pressure, fear, and worry* in the providence of God. Knowing that God is the sovereign ruler over the entire universe, we can find comfort in an unpredictable world. We need not live with worldly fear (Psa. 91:5-6). Jesus tells us, "Do not worry," precisely because God takes care of the birds and the lilies, and all the things we need (food and clothing) will be added to us (Matt. 6:25-34). Paul wrote, "But godliness with contentment is great gain…and having food and clothing, with these we shall be content" (1 Tim. 6:6, 8). God's providence comforts and calms the troubled soul.

The Christian learns to *trust* God in all things because of divine providence. When Eli was told of the judgment that was coming to his home due to the evil of his sons, he said in humility and trust, "It is the Lord. Let Him do what seems good to Him" (1 Sam. 3:18). David said of God, "Here I am, let Him do to me as seems good to Him" (2 Sam. 15:26). This demonstrates full submission and trust in God. Job observed, "The Lord gave, and the Lord has taken away; blessed be the name of the Lord" (Job 1:21). Job would later say, "Though He slay me, yet will I trust Him" (13:15). What faith and trust in the worst of circumstances! Great confidence this gives us, for "it is an incomparable blessing to be able to reflect upon the providence of God and upon the sovereignty of his rule over the universe. In light of all we know about his providential control, we can trust the future into his hands with the utmost confidence."[12]

The Christian also understands that his *choices* day by day have very real consequences in his life. Choices about friends, a college major, marriage partner, job, neighborhood, and church will resonate with positive and negative results depending on the wisdom of those choices. The most important choice of all will be to become a Christian. Our choices will either help us to be open to hear God's word and follow his will, or ignore his word and follow this corrupt world and its desires. A modern proverb says "God helps those who help themselves." Make good choices and God will assist you through his divine spiritual and physical providence.

CONCLUSION

The providence of God is a vast and intriguing subject, full of wondrous and comforting truths for the faithful child of God. God provides so much for mankind each and every day, and has special care for his spiritual children in Christ. In this world of sin and sorrow, let us pray in faith, work in truth, and hope in love as we submit to the sovereign ruler of the universe. God is working in this world as time counts down to the final day of salvation. Live faithfully and commit yourself to his service, so that God may use you for his purposes in saving men and bringing glory to himself for all eternity.

God is in charge; the presumptuous principalities and powers of this world are no match for the sovereign lordship of the Creator and Ruler of the universe. This is the basis of our confidence even in the face of adversity....[13]

❧ QUESTIONS ❧

1. Why is God's providence difficult to recognize? _____
   _____
   _____

2. Give your own short definition of divine providence. _____
   _____
   _____

3. What does "general providence" have reference to? _____
   _____
   _____

4. In what ways does God provide for the existence of the earth and its inhabitants? _____
   _____
   _____

5. What does "special providence" have reference to? _____
   _____
   _____

6. What does Paul mean that "all things work together for good to those who love God"? _____
   _____
   _____
   _____

7. How was God responsible for Joseph being in Egypt? _____
   _____
   _____

8. How did God use Esther to save the Jewish people? _____
   _____
   _____

9. How can God influence us without interfering with our free choices? ____
   _____
   _____

10. What is the ultimate goal of God's providential work? _____
_____
_____

11. Why should we not blame God for all the bad things that happen to us? _____
_____
_____

12. How can I know that God loves me if my life is going so badly? ____
_____
_____

13. How will prayer help our daily lives? _____
_____
_____

14. What should be our reaction when tragedy occurs? _____
_____
_____

15. List some positive responses of the Christian to the providence of God. _____
_____
_____

Fill in the Blank and Give the Scripture

1. "Your _____ be done" (_____)

2. "Look at the _____ of the air, for they neither _____ nor _____ nor gather into barns; yet your heavenly _____ _____ them" (_____)

3. "And he changes the _____ and the _____; He removes _____ and raises up _____" (_____)

4. "Though he _____, he shall not be utterly cast down; for the Lord _____ him with His _____" (_____)

5. "...do not therefore be _____ or angry with yourselves because you _____ me here; for _____ sent me before you to preserve _____" (_____)

6. "Yet who knows whether you have _____ to the kingdom for such a _____ as this?" (_____)

7. "The effective, fervent _____ of a _____ man avails _____" (_____)

8. "Your _____ I have hidden in my _____, that I may not _____ against You" (_____)

9. "...you ought to say, 'If the Lord _____, we shall _____ and do this and that" (_____)

10. "It is the _____. Let Him ____ what seems _____ to Him" (_____)

TRUE OR FALSE

1. ___ The providence of God describes how God performs miracles on our behalf.
2. ___ God is aware and involved in the affairs of men and nations to-day.
3. ___ Special providence refers to God's care and supervision over the created universe.
4. ___ Joseph never understood why he ended up in Egypt.
5. ___ Esther was willing to die to try and save her people.
6. ___ If I choose to step off a cliff, it is God's fault if something bad happens.
7. ___ How God answers my prayer is decided by God himself.
8. ___ If I am a Christian, God will keep me from ever suffering through any tragedy.
9. ___ A humble, godly life will not help me live a safer, healthier, and longer life.
10. ___ God's providence helps us overcome earthly fears, pressures, and worries.

THOUGHT QUESTIONS

1. List some specific truths (principles, warnings, commands) that God reveals in his word that will help a person live a life that is healthier, safer, longer, and happier.

2. Why should a Christian still pray for the sick to recover, those traveling to be safe, and the lost to obey the gospel if there is no absolute guarantee that it will happen?

3. How does the providence of God make us stronger as we encounter and experience the evil and suffering of this present world (consider 2 Cor. 12:7-10 and Jas. 5:10-11)?

MISCONCEPTIONS ABOUT GOD

In Psalm 50:21, God said, "These things you have done, and I kept silent; you thought that I was altogether like you." Because God had not punished these sinners immediately, they thought that he approved of their wicked ways.[1] They had misjudged God for he said, "But I will reprove you, and set them in order before your eyes" (v. 21b). They were in grave danger of God tearing them in pieces like a lion would its prey and "there be none to deliver" (v. 22).

Many people today mistakenly think that God thinks and feels as they do. They foolishly believe that God approves, or disapproves, whatever they approve or disapprove. They measure God with themselves as the standard. This erroneous human standard causes them to be ignorant of the true nature of God and to develop false concepts of God. What is created is a god fashioned after man's heart, which is idolatry (cf. Rom. 1:22, 23).

God's thoughts and ways are higher than man's "as the heavens are higher than the earth" (Isa. 55:8, 9). God's judgment of others is often different from man's judgment. "For the Lord does not see as man sees; for man looks at the outward appearance, but the Lord looks at the heart" (1 Sam. 16:7). "For what is highly esteemed among men is an abomination in the sight of God" (Lk. 16:15). Men may sincerely believe that they are following a way that leads to heaven, but sadly discover in the judgment that it was "the way of death" (Prov. 14:12).

IDOLS ARE THE PRODUCT OF MAN'S IMAGINATION

Idols are man's vain attempts to make their gods conform to their way of thinking. Idolaters made their gods in their own image by attributing their own sinful ways to them such as: lying, adultery, murder, jealousy, greed, etc. "The Greeks made their gods in their own image... He [Zeus, *drh*] is represented as falling in love with one woman after another and descending to all manner of tricks to hide his infidelity from his wife."[2] While we do not worship material idols, our concepts about God may be just as distorted as theirs.

Many Mistakenly Think that God:

Is a Racial God
God is not white, red, brown, or any other color. He does not possess flesh for "God is Spirit" (Jn. 4:24). He is the Creator of us all (Acts 17:24-28). He loves everyone and strongly desires their soul's salvation (Jn. 3:16; 1 Tim. 2:3, 4). He does not possess any racial prejudice: "For there is no partiality with God" (Rom. 2:11). Peter finally realized this while preaching the gospel to Gentiles (Acts 10:9-35). To be like him, we must not show respect of persons (Jas. 2:1-9).

Jonah was exceedingly angry with God for not destroying more than 120,000 Assyrians. Because they repented of their evil ways, "God relented from the disaster that He said He would bring upon them" (Jonah 3:10). We should all rejoice that God is a "gracious and merciful God, slow to anger and abundant in lovingkindness, One who relents from doing harm" (4:2).

Is Dead
God is not subject to disease or death since he is "Spirit" (Jn. 4:24). He is eternal: "Even from everlasting to everlasting, You are God" (Psa. 90:2). There never was a time that God did not exist and there never will be a time when he does not exist. God said his name is "I AM WHO I AM" (Ex. 3:14). His name is not "I WAS" or "I WILL BE" for he used the present tense verb "AM." He does not have birthdays for he was never born.

Mary gave birth to Jesus to give him a body of flesh (Lk. 2:7). Jesus became incarnate for he had to put on a body of flesh so he could die on a cross (Phil. 2:6-8; Heb. 2:14; 10:5). The word "incarnate" means, "endowed with a human body."[3]

Is Growing Old and Feeble
Since God is eternal, he does not grow old and feeble. He is not bound by time (2 Pet. 3:8). He does not grow weary from being exhausted. "The

Creator of the ends of the earth neither faints nor is weary" (Isa. 40:28). He doesn't need to renew his strength by resting. "He rested on the seventh day from all His work which He had done" because he had ceased his work of creation (Gen. 2:1-3).

It is very irreverent to refer to the Almighty God as "the old man upstairs." We must always speak to him, and about him, with heart-felt reverence. Never speak his holy name in vain (Ex. 20:7). The Lord said, "My name is blasphemed continually every day" (Isa. 52:5). Sadly, such is still true today.

FORGETS HIS PROMISES

Peter wrote that some scoffers would ask, "Where is the promise of His coming?" (2 Pet. 3:3-4). Peter's inspired answer was, "The Lord is not slack concerning His promise..." (2 Pet. 3:9). The writer of Hebrews wrote, "He who promised is faithful" (10:23). Paul wrote, "For all the promises of God in Him are Yes, and in Him Amen" (2 Cor. 1:20). Joshua said that God had kept all his promises to Israel concerning the land of Canaan (Josh. 23:14). Jesus will come again as he promised (Jn. 14:3).

We may fail to keep our promises because: 1. we have made promises beyond our ability to keep as politicians often do, 2. circumstances may change making it impossible for us to keep them, 3. we may decide that it is too much effort, or expense, to keep them, or, 4. we forget them. God's promises are not affected by any of these things. Therefore, we can stand upon his promises.

WILL FORGET THEIR SINS FOR WHICH THEY HAVE NOT REPENTED

The passing of time often causes us to forget many things. As we grow older our memory often fades. Sadly, many have forgotten God (Psa. 50:22). The Psalmist spoke of how the wicked man views God and his own sin: "God has forgotten; He hides His face; He will never see it" (Psa. 10:3-11). Many are like the Gentiles who "did not like to retain God in their knowledge" (Rom. 1:28). The Jews were often warned, "Beware that you do not forget the Lord your God..." (Deut. 8:11-20). However, they did forget God (Judg. 3:7; Jer. 2:32; 3:21).

Forgetting God shows that we are ungrateful for the wonderful blessings which he has given us. Forgetting to worship God is fatal to our soul's eternal life (Psa. 9:17). God will not remember our sins if we will obey his conditions of forgiveness (Acts 2:38; Rom. 10:9, 10; 1 Jn. 1:9; Heb. 8:12).

CAN LIE
If one believes that Jesus never lived or was only a good man, but not the Son of God, then such a one must believe that the Father and Son lied (Matt. 3:17; 16:16, 17). God cannot lie (Tit. 1:2). It is contrary to his holy nature. God hates lying! In Proverbs 6:16-19, it is stated that seven things "are an abomination to Him." Among those seven things are "a lying tongue" and "a false witness who speaks lies." Balaam said, "God is not a man, that He should lie, nor a son of man, that He should repent" (Num. 23:16). If man contradicts what God has said, man is the one that is lying (Rom. 3:4). Since God cannot lie, his word is truth (Jn. 17:17). We can have complete confidence in the truthfulness of the Bible.

Lying has become very prominent in our society. We have been conditioned to believe that much of what we hear is lies. The Psalmist wrote, "I said in my haste, all men are liars" (Psa. 116:11). If we are guilty of lying, we must repent or we will be eternally "in the lake which burns with fire and brimstone" (Rev. 21:8).

CAN BE DECEIVED
It is a grave mistake to believe that because we can be deceived, and are capable of deceiving others, that God can be deceived. God cannot be deceived! "Do not be deceived. God is not mocked; for whatever a man sows, that will he also reap. For he who sows to his flesh will of the flesh reap corruption, but he who sows to the Spirit will of the Spirit reap everlasting life" (Gal. 6:7, 8).

It is an unbroken universal law, in both the physical and spiritual realm, that we reap what we sow. We cannot sow "to the flesh" and "reap everlasting life." Ananias and Sapphira lied about the amount they received from the sale of their land (Acts 5:1-3). God was not deceived and caused them to die (vv. 4-11). Since God cannot be mocked, we must not make a mockery of being a Christian. We must not pretend to be faithful Christians, while we sing feebly, give sparingly, and worship infrequently. There will be no hypocrites in heaven!

CAN BE BRIBED
Because God is "a just God," he cannot be bribed (Isa. 45:21). God asked the Jews, who had forsaken him, "To what purpose is the multitude of

your sacrifices to Me?" (Isa. 1:2-11). He despised their sacrifices, worship services, and prayers because their hands were "full of blood" (Isa. 1:12-15). To be in his favor again, they must "cease to do evil, learn to do good, seek justice..." (Isa. 1:16, 17). Justice has often been perverted by the taking of bribes (Amos 5:12). The prophet, Samuel, did not take bribes, but his sons did (1 Sam. 8:3; 12:3).

It has been said, "Everyone has their price." We must not be willing to do something sinful regardless of the amount of money offered to us. An honest person does not have a "love of money" (1 Tim. 6:10).

God does not overlook our sins because we: 1. Often come to worship services, 2. do good deeds, or 3. give liberally to his church. For a Christian to receive God's forgiveness, he must repent and confess his sins with a "broken and contrite heart" (Acts 17:30; 1 Jn. 1:9; Psa. 51:17).

DOES NOT LOOK UPON SIN AS SOMETHING TERRIBLE

Some want to engage in sinful activities, but they do not want their conscience to condemn them so they convince themselves that God will not punish them for their sins because he either approves, or is indifferent, to their sins. Many want their "god" to allow them to live as they please. They have become so accustomed to sin that they are no longer shocked and repulsed by it. They assume that God has also become tolerant of sin.

God is grieved to see our pure souls, which he created in his image, corrupted by our sins (Gen. 6:5, 6). Sin separates us from his blessed fellowship (Isa. 59:1, 2; 1 Jn. 1:5, 6). Our sins will cause us to be horribly punished eternally in "the lake with burns with fire and brimstone" (Rev. 21:8). We should hate the destructive consequences of sin in our lives and the lives of others (Psa. 97:10; Rom. 6:23; 12:9)!

Sin is so horrible in God's eyes that he gave his Son to die a very painful death on a cross even though his Son pleaded with him "let this cup pass from Me" (Jn. 3:16; Matt. 26:39). Jesus was the perfect sacrificial Lamb. He died so his precious blood could remove sin from our souls in baptism (Matt. 26:28; Acts 22:16).

IS MEAN, CRUEL, AND DELIGHTS IN PUNISHING MAN

Because God's wrath has fallen upon man in times past, some have come to the false conclusion that he enjoys inflicting pain and suffering on man. God did cause a great flood to drown all except "eight souls" (Gen. 6, 7;

1 Pet. 3:20). He did rain "brimstone and fire on Sodom and Gomorrah" because their sin was "very grievous" (Gen. 18:20; 19:24).

However, God would much rather forgive our sins than punish us for them. "But You are God, ready to pardon, gracious and merciful, slow to anger, abundant in kindness, and did not forsake them" (Neh. 9:17). We should be very grateful that God does not delight in our suffering! He encourages us to cast our "care upon Him, for He cares" for us (1 Pet. 5:7). Through Jesus, our "great High Priest," we may "come boldly to the throne of grace that we may obtain mercy and find grace to help in time of need" (Heb. 4:14-16).

God has "no pleasure in the death of the wicked" (Ezek. 33:11). He admonishes his children, "Do not rejoice when your enemy falls, and do not let your heart be glad when he stumbles" (Prov. 24:17). Many find it difficult to be like their heavenly Father by having this attitude toward their enemies. He does not beat us into submission, but wants us to be devoted to him because of his "goodness, forbearance, and longsuffering" toward us (Rom. 2:4).

God wants us to be reconciled with him. The word, "reconcile" means, "To bring back to friendship after estrangement."[4] How wonderful that he took the initiative in providing a way of reconciliation through the death of Jesus in the shedding of his blood which removes sin from our souls (2 Cor. 5:18-21). He wants all to be saved from the torments of hell (1 Tim. 2:3, 4; 2 Pet. 3:9).

"IS LOVE" AND WILL NOT PUNISH ANYONE ETERNALLY IN HELL

Jehovah's Witnesses do not believe in the existence of hell.[5] I had one of their members try to convince me that hell does not exist using the following argument. He said, "No matter how awful your children behaved would you throw them in a fire?" I answered, "No." He asked, "Do you believe that Jehovah's love far exceeds yours?" I said, "Yes." Then he said, "How can you believe that Jehovah will throw his children in a lake of fire?" This line of reasoning is a good example of making God in man's image by holding him to a human standard.

Jesus warned many times of the horrible punishment that awaits the sinner in hell (Matt. 5:22, 29, 30; 10:28; 23:33). The Bible clearly teaches, "And anyone not found written in the Book of Life was cast into the lake of fire" (Rev. 20:15). Revelation 21:8 gives a partial list of those who "shall have their part in the lake which burns with fire and brimstone, which is the second death."

Denying the existence of hell will not cause it to cease to exist. God wants the sinner warned about the eternal punishment waiting for him after the judgment so he will be motivated to obey God's conditions of forgiveness and not experience the horrors of hell. If there was no punishment for failure to obey God's commandments, then his commandments would be ignored.

DOES NOT KNOW THEIR SECRET SINS
Some mistakenly think that since they have successfully hidden their wickedness from men, they have hidden their sins from God. Achan hid his theft from men, but not from God (Josh. 7). "The eyes of the Lord are in every place, keeping watch on the evil and the good" (Prov. 15:3). "And there is no creature hidden from His sight, but all things are naked and open to the eyes of Him to whom we must give account" (Heb. 4:13).

God can see as well in the darkness as in the light (Psa. 139:7-12). He even knows your thoughts (Psa. 94:11; Matt. 9:4). You shall give account in the judgment "for every idle word" (Matt. 12:36). "For God will bring every work into judgment, including every secret thing, whether it is good or whether it is evil" (Eccl. 12:14).

WILL ALLOW ONE TO DISOBEY HIM IF IT MAKES ONE HAPPY
Some foolishly reason, "Since God wants me to be happy, I can disregard his laws which keep me from being happy." Some apply this faulty reasoning to remarriage when they do not have scriptural grounds for remarriage (Matt. 19:9). Some want to find sexual pleasure outside of marriage (Heb. 13:4). Therefore, they deceive themselves into believing that God will not condemn them for being sexually immoral (1 Cor. 6:9, 10, 18). No one, who is accountable, is exempt from obeying all of God's laws for he does not show partiality (Rom. 2:11; Jas. 2:10).

APPROVES OF ALL RELIGIOUS DENOMINATIONS
Many thank God for establishing many different religious denominations so one may choose the church of their choice. They believe, since one church is as good as another, it does not matter which church they choose to join. They believe that there are saved people in all churches. These are popular beliefs. Where is the scripture upon which these beliefs are founded?

The Bible clearly teaches that God does not approve of denominationalism for it involves religious division. Religious division is condemned by God (1 Cor. 1:10-13)! Jesus said, "I will build My church" (Matt. 16:18). Notice Jesus did not say, "I will build My churches." Jesus said, "...there will be one flock and one shepherd" (Jn. 10:16). He prayed for unity among his followers (Jn. 17:20-23). He wants all Christians united in "one body" and have "one faith" (Eph. 4:4, 5).

God disapproves of denominational churches for they have been established by men. They did not originate in Jerusalem on the first Pentecost after the Lord's resurrection (Acts 2). They came into existence hundreds of years later. They are called by names never applied to the church one reads about in the New Testament. They offer vain worship for they teach "as doctrines the commandments of men" (Matt. 15:7-9). For example, where does the Bible teach that Jesus was born on Christmas? They give people a false sense of security about the salvation of their souls. For example, they teach that baptism is not necessary for the forgiveness of one's sins. Jesus clearly made baptism an essential condition for one's salvation from the penalty of sin. "He who believes and is baptized will be saved; but he who does not believe will be condemned" (Mk. 16:16).

It would be wonderful, as God desires it to be, if all who claim to be Christians were united in the church belonging to Christ (Rom. 16:16). The Lord wills "that you all speak the same thing and that there be no divisions among you, but that you be perfectly joined together in the same mind and in the same judgment" (1 Cor. 1:10). Such unity could exist if all were willing to "abide in the doctrine of Christ" (2 Jn. 9).

CONCLUSION

ONLY THE BIBLE GIVES TRUE CONCEPTS OF GOD

Our concepts of the nature and character of God are the most important concepts we possess. "What a man thinks in his heart of God is the turning-point of life and character."[6] Let us make sure that our thoughts and ideas of God are founded on the truthfulness of his word.

To avoid any misconceptions about God, we must open our hearts to seek the truth revealed by God about himself in the Scriptures. False concepts about God will only create false idols of human ignorance. Let us turn "to God from idols to serve the living and true God" (1 Thess. 1:9).

✺ QUESTIONS ✺

1. In Psalm 50:16-21, why did the wicked think that God would not punish them for their sins? _____

   _____

   _____

2. Sinners are in grave danger of God doing what to them (Psa. 50:22)?

   _____

   _____

3. Does God approve, or disapprove, whatever we approve or disapprove? _____

   _____

4. How much higher are God's ways and thoughts than ours? _____

   _____

   _____

5. What color is God? Explain. _____

   _____

   _____

6. Why is it impossible for God to die? _____

   _____

   _____

7. Why did Jesus put on a body of flesh? _____

   _____

   _____

8. Has God ever been sick or tired? _____

   _____

9. What does it mean that God "rested from His work"? _____

   _____

   _____

10. When God makes an unconditional promise, are there any circumstances that may arise to keep him from keeping that promise? _____

   _____

   _____

11. What removes sin from our souls?_____
    (give scripture _____)

12. When is sin removed from the soul of the non-Christian? _____
    _____ (give scripture _____)

13. What separates us from God's fellowship? _____
    _____

14. Should we rejoice when something bad happens to our enemies? ___
    _____
    _____

15. What does "reconcile" mean? _____
    _____

16. Who took the initiative in reconciling God and man? _____
    _____
    _____

17. Who spoke often about the existence of hell? _____
    _____
    _____

18. Does God know your thoughts?_____
    (give scripture_____)

19. When will every secret be revealed? _____
    _____

20. Where is the scripture that teaches that God approves of all religious
    denominations? _____
    _____

21. What is our most important concept? _____
    _____

FILL IN THE BLANK

1. God's judgment is different from man's because he _____ on
   the _____ and man looks at the _____ _____ (give
   scripture _____)

2. God cannot _____ (give the scripture _____).

3. God cannot be _____ (Galatians _____).

4. Since God is a just God, he cannot be _____.

5. Many want their _____ to allow them to live as they _____.

6. God wants _____ to be _____. (1 Tim. _____).

7. "The _____ of the _____ are in every _____." (give scripture _____)

8. Denominationalism involves _____ _____.

9. "He who _____ and is _____ will be _____" (give scripture _____)

Match the Verse with the Correct Scripture Reference

1. ___ "For the Lord does not see as man sees"   a. Numbers 23:19
2. ___ "For there is no partiality with God"   b. 1 Samuel 16:7
3. ___ "Even from everlasting to everlasting, You are God"   c. Isaiah 1:11
4. ___ "God is not a man, that He should lie"   d. Romans 2:11
5. ___ "To what purpose is the multitude of your
      sacrifices to Me"   e. Isaiah 40:28
6. ___ "The Creator of the ends of the earth,
      neither faints nor is weary"   f. Psalm 90:2

True or False

1. ___ God does not look on sin as terrible.
2. ___ God delights in punishing us.
3. ___ God will not punish anyone eternally in hell.
4. ___ If your name is not in the Book of Life, you will be cast into hell.
5. ___ God wants the sinner warned about hell.
6. ___ God can see in the darkness.
7. ___ It is alright to disobey God if it makes you happy.
8. ___ Jesus prayed for all disciples to be united.
9. ___ The Bible teaches that Jesus was born on Christmas.

THOUGHT QUESTIONS

1. What proves how much God hates sin?

2. Why does God's love for sinners not prevent him from casting the wicked into hell?

3. How can one be reconciled with God?

4. List several reasons why God does not approve of denominational churches.

FOOTNOTES

LESSON 1
[1] The specific term for the study of God is theology, a combination of two Greek words: theos (God) and logos (the study of). Sometimes the term theology is used more broadly to include all religious studies or a particular field of religious study.

[2] Aude McKee, "How Men Come to Know God," Guardian of Truth, 1985 January 17, 16.

[3] All Bible quotes are from the New Kings James Version unless otherwise noted.

[4] Jack Cottrell, What the Bible Says About God the Creator, 5. Cottrell goes on to discuss the fact that true worship and morality is dependent on a knowledge of God (5-6).

[5] Curtis Dickson, quoted in Cottrell, op. cit., 16.

[6] McKee, op. cit., 17.

[7] Funk & Wagnalls Standard Dictionary, International edition, Vol. 1, 475.

[8] Ibid., 648.

[9] Charles Hodge, A Biblical Study of God, 8-9.

[10] James D. Bales, The Biblical Doctrine of God, 5.

LESSON 2
[1] Martin Rose, "Names of God in the OT," The Anchor Bible Dictionary, Vol. 4, 1002.

[2] Young's Analytical Concordance to the Bible, 8.

[3] Ibid., 835.

[4] D. W. Baker, "God, Names of," Dictionary of the Old Testament: Pentateuch, 359-360.

[5] Nathan Stone, Names of God, 9.

[6] Robert J. Wyatt, "God, Names of," The International Standard Bible Encyclopedia, Rev. ed., Vol. 2, 505; Mike Willis notes that "their derivation in Hebrew is not absolutely known, although many scholars suggest that they are derived from a root which means 'to be strong'" ("The Names of God," Guardian of Truth, 1985 January 17, 2).

[7] Synonyms of the Old Testament, 22.

[8] Though the word "trinity" is not in the Bible, the concept of three persons equally sharing the essence and nature of deity is revealed throughout the Scriptures (see Lesson 5 "The Triune Nature of God").

[9] "Tetragrammaton" means "having four letters."

[10] Do these passages about the patriarchs knowing the name Yahweh contradict Exodus 6:3: "..but by My name Yahweh I was not known to them"? Liberal critics would like to think so, but their interpretation ignores how a known name can be given a special meaning at a later time. Henry Cowles explains: "The meaning is, not that the name Jehovah was never used by them or given of God to them: but that its special significance had not been manifested to them as He was now about to make it manifest" (quoted in John J. Davis, Moses and the Gods of Egypt: Studies in Exodus, 85).

[11] Wyatt, op. cit., 506.

[12] Ibid., 507. "Sometimes it is to be read as adonay, with this word's vowels appended to the consonants yhwh (i.e., yeh[o]wah, from which we get 'Jehovah' through the more archaic English pronunciation of the letters)," Baker, op. cit., 365. The Jehovah's Witnesses are wrong to insist that "Jehovah" is the only translation of the name of God that should be used. Most modern English versions translate yahweh as "LORD" in small capitals.

[13] Most of the passages cited here use all three of the major names for God. For example, Exodus 34:23: "Three times in the year all your men shall appear before the Lord [adonay], the LORD [yahweh] God [elohim] of Israel."

[14] Mike Willis, "Names of God," Guardian of Truth, 1985 January 17, 22.

[15] This scriptural fact is devastating to the false doctrine of the Jehovah's Witnesses that denies that Jesus is deity, equal to the Father. Jesus is the I AM and identified by all the major names of God.

LESSON 3
[1] Langdon Gilkey, quoted in Jack Cottrell, What the Bible Says About God the Creator, 95.
[2] Bobby Witherington, "The Works of God," Guardian of Truth, 1985 January 17, 14.
[3] Nelson's Expository Dictionary of the Old Testament, 84.
[4] John J. Davis, Paradise to Prison: Studies in Genesis, 41.
[5] "Light" is visible electromagnetic radiation necessary for plant photosynthesis, among other uses. The sun was later created as a specific generator of light. As Henry M. Morris writes, "On the first day, He had said: 'Let there be light!' (Hebrew or). On the fourth day, He said: 'Let there be lights' (or light-givers, Hebrew ma-or). Intrinsic light first, then generators of light later, is both the logical and the Biblical order" (The Genesis Record, 65).
[6] "This statement seems to confirm the fact that 'firmament' and 'heaven' are essentially synonymous terms, both meaning 'space' – either space in general or a particular region of space, depending on context" (Ibid., 58).
[7] A. O. Schnabel, Has God Spoken, 14-15.
[8] "The second chapter of Genesis describes in greater detail certain of the events of the sixth day of creation, especially of the formation of the first man and woman. It does not in any respect contradict the account in the first chapter, but instead is complementary to it" (Morris, Ibid., 83).
[9] Some popular theories of men that deny that the days of creation were literal, consecutive, and sequential 24-hour days are the Gap Theory (gap of millions of years between Gen. 1:1 and Gen. 1:2), the Day-Age Theory (days are ages of millions of years), Literal Day-Long Gap Theory (millions of years pass between the creative days), and the Framework Hypothesis (days are part of a non-literal, symbolic "story" of creation). These theories deny the literal, historical language and structure of Genesis, and are dangerous compromises designed to force a twisted interpretation of Genesis 1 that will accommodate the fallacious timetables of geological and biological evolutionary theory. (For more information on this important subject, see The Days of Creation by Dan King)
[10] Ferrell Jenkins, The Scheme of Redemption (Part 1), Truth in Life workbook series, 34.
[11] John N. Clayton, "The Sun and Its Design," Evidences of God, 109.
[12] Funk & Wagnalls Standard Dictionary, International Edition, Vol. 2, 1457.
[13] "If...the lunar size were increased to just twice the present diameter, the magnitude of earth tides would be increased by a factor of eight" (John C. Whitcomb and Donald B. DeYoung, The Moon: Its Creation, Form and Significance, 140).
[14] John Clayton, "Probability and Chance in Creation, Evidences of God, 164-166.
[15] Batsell Barrett Baxter, I Believe Because..., 54. See also Bill Cooper, Paley's Watchmaker.

Lesson 4
[1] Funk & Wagnalls Standard Dictionary, International Edition, Vol. 1, 101.
[2] James Bales, The Biblical Doctrine of God, 10.
[3] John Clayton, "New Data On 'Big Bang Theory' Putting Clinching Arguments on God's Creation," Evidence of God, 74-75 (For more information on the "Big Bang Theory" see Time magazine, Dec. 4, 1995).
[4] Funk and Wagnall, op. cit., 441.
[5] John W. Klotz, quoted in John L. Clark and David A. Eakin, The Theory of Evolution and Special Creation, 2.

[6] Peter J. Wilson, Indestructible Foundations, 10.

[7] Charles Darwin himself admitted that the lack of intermediate, transitional fossils was a huge problem for his theory. In his book The Origin of Species, after asserting that an "enormous" amount of intermediate links once existed on the earth, he asked, "Why then is not every geological formation and every stratum full of such intermediate links? Geology assuredly does not reveal any such finely graduated organic chain; and this, perhaps, is the most obvious and gravest objection which can be urged against my theory" (292).

[8] Duane T. Gish, Evoluton: The Fossils Still Say NO!, 356.

[9] Ibid.

[10] Ibid., 357.

[11] Jenkins, The Scheme of Redemption (Part 1), Truth in Life workbook series, 31.

[12] Batsell Barrett Baxter, I Believe Because..., 91.

[13] Clayton, "Does God Exist," Vol. 37, No. 5, Sept-Oct. 2010, 12-13.

[14] The Bible is not a scientific textbook, but where it touches upon scientific matters, it speaks accurately (e.g. life in the blood, Gen. 9:4; Lev. 17:14).

[15] Funk & Wagnall, op. cit., 139.

[16] John N. Moore, Questions and Answers on Creation/Evolution, 35.

[17] "The evolutionists' imagined integration of molecules into planets and later into living substance, and finally into humankind, is in complete violation of the first and second laws of thermodynamics" (Ibid.)

[18] Funk & Wagnall, op. cit., 590.

[19] Even Charles Darwin admitted that the complexity of life forms could disprove his theory of natural selection: "If it could be demonstrated that any complex organ existed, which could not possibly have been formed by numerous, successive, slight modifications, my theory would absolutely break down" (The Origin of Species, 219). The complex physical processes of reproduction and birth, along with the critical respiratory and cardiovascular systems, break down Darwin's theory in favor of special creation by God.

[20] Baxter, op. cit., 159.

[21] Clayton, "Theistic Evolution," op. cit., 119-120.

[22] Gordon Wilson, Theistic Evolution, 37. See also Bert Thompson, Theistic Evolution, 213-235.

[23] Tony Woods, "The Atheist Lifestyle, Not Christianity, Is For the Weak," The Lakeland Ledger, 29 November 2009 (letters to the editor).

[24] Luther Blackmon, God or Evolution? (tract), 2.

[25] Baxter, op. cit., 81.

LESSON 5

[1] Our finite understanding of God is limited to what has been revealed in Scripture. One would have to be God himself to fully comprehend the triune nature of God. As Jack Cottrell states, "...there is mystery associated with the doctrine of the Trinity. We may have some true understanding of it, but we cannot understand it fully" (God the Redeemer, 150).

[2] The term "triune" is preferred over "trinity" in this study, though they are nearly synonymous in their dictionary definitions. "Triune" is a descriptive term meaning "three in one" or a unity of three, as the one God is described in the Bible. "Trinity" is often used as a theological term that is given various meanings depending on the creedal explanation of a particular religious group.

[3] This verse is called the Shema by Jews, named after the Hebrew word for "hear."

[4] A chapter on Hinduism in a college textbook used by the author is entitled "Three Hundred and Thirty Million Gods (A Study of Hinduism)."

[5] Wicca is a pantheistic ("all is God"), as well as a polytheistic, religion. It sees the universe ("nature") as being a pantheon of gods and goddesses. Modern New Age philosophies are quite similar.

[6] Be careful not to be deceived by "tritheism" (a form of polytheism) which contends that three separate spirit essences exist as three distinct Gods, unified only by a common will and purpose (for more on this see Lanier, The Timeless Trinity for the Ceaseless Centuries, 47-48).

[7] Roy H. Lanier, Sr. The Timeless Trinity for the Ceaseless Centuries, 45, 46.

[8] Webster's New Universal Unabridged Dictionary, 526.

[9] Ibid., 931.

[10] Richard C. Trench, Synonyms of the New Testament, 8.

[11] Ibid.

[12] W. E. Vine, An Expository Dictionary of New Testament Words, Vol. 1, 328.

[13] This sharing of an equal nature while maintaining a difference in role and work could be illustrated by the familiar structure of a family. While all members of a family are equal in nature (humanity), there are separate roles of authority/subjection (husband/wife; parent/child) and work (provider/keeper of home).

[14] "This passage reflects oneness as well as threeness, since only one name is mentioned. This indicates an essential equality as well as equal significance in the bestowing of salvation" (Cottrell, op. cit, 130).

[15] It is worth noting that some older versions contain the following words in 1 John 5:7: "the Father, the Word, and the Holy Spirit; and these three are one." Although the extensive manuscript evidence shows this to be an uninspired gloss (addition) to the text, it does reflect the truth taught throughout the New Testament (for more information, see Daniel H. King, Sr. The Three Epistles of John, 154-157).

[16] Mormonism is a polytheistic religion: "Mormon theology then is polytheistic, teaching in effect that the universe is inhabited by different gods who procreate spirit children which are in turn clothed with bodies on different planets, 'Elohim' being the god of this planet..." (Walter Martin, Kingdom of the Cults, 204). Faithful Mormons believe that they will eventually become gods equal to those that now exist.

[17] Should You Believe in the Trinity?, 14, 16.

[18] See William D. Mounce, Complete Expository Dictionary of Old & New Testament Words, 255.

[19] Robert Harkrider, Revelation, 22.

[20] Should You Believe in the Trinity?, 20, 23.

[21] Gene Frost, The "Oneness" Doctrine of Pentecostalism and the Bible Doctrine of the Godhead, 4.

Lesson 6

[1] Webster's New Universal Unabridged Dictionary, 1351.

[2] See Lesson 2, "The Names of God."

[3] The things that the Bible says God "cannot" do (lie – Tit. 1:2; be tempted by evil – Jas. 1:13) do not reveal weakness on God's part. Rather, such things are a contradiction of his nature. God can do anything that is consistent with his will. For example, God has the power to destroy an evil world with a flood, but it is not his will to do it again (Gen. 9:11).

[4] Jack Cottrell, What the Bible Says About God the Creator, 255.

5 Allan Turner, The Christian & Idolatry, 23.

6 Weldon E. Warnock, "The Omnipresent God," Guardian of Truth, 1985 January 17, 11.

7 Turner, op. cit.

8 Warnock, op. cit., 12.

9 Cottrell, op. cit., 283-284; Roy Lanier stated it this way: "God's foreknowledge of a man's choice of a course in life has nothing to do with the man's freedom to choose his own course" (The Timeless Trinity, 145).

10 Cottrell, op. cit., 305.

LESSON 7

1 The Zondervan Pictorial Bible Dictionary, Merrill C. Tenney, Gen. ed., 316.

2 Ron Carlson and Ed Decker, Fast Facts on False Teachings, 171.

3 Ibid,, 170.

4 Ibid., 165.

5 Funk & Wagnalls Standard Dictionary, International edition, Vol. 1, 63.

6 James Bales, The Biblical Doctrine of God, 19.

7 Ibid., 26.

8 Funk & Wagnalls Standard Dictionary, Vol. 2, 882.

9 Bales, op. cit., 32.

10 See Lesson Six, The "All" Power, Knowledge, and Presence of God.

11 Zondervan, op. cit., 357.

12 "...the best understanding of the Old Testament word for holy is that it means 'to cut, to separate' in its verb form. Thus to say that something is holy means that it is separated or set off from other things" (Jack Cottrell, What the Bible Says About God the Redeemer, 246).

13 W. E. Vine, An Expository Dictionary of New Testament Words, Vol. 2, 225.

14 J. C. Lambert, "Holiness," The International Standard Bible Encyclopedia, James Orr, gen. ed. Vol. 3, 1403-1404.

15 Cottrell, op. cit., 246-247, 250.

16 Zondevan, op. cit., 751.

17 Vine, Vol. 3, 317,

18 Roy Lanier, Sr. The Timeless Trinity for the Ceaseless Centuries, 103.

LESSON 8

1 D. Edmond Hiebert, "Love," Zondervan Pictorial Dictionary, 493.

2 Jack Cottrell, What the Bible Says About God the Redeemer, 399.

3 Funk and Wagnalls Standard Dictionary, International edition, Vol. 1, 754-755.

4 William Evans, "Love," Vol. 3, 1932.

5 James Bales, The Biblical Doctrine of God, 65.

6 W. E.. Vine, Expository Dictionary of New Testament Words, Vol. 3, 21.

7 Larry Ray Hafley, The Love of God, Guardian of Truth, Vol. 29, No. 2, 5.

8 International Standard Bible Encyclopedia, op. cit.

9 Guy N. Woods, A Commentary on the New Testament Epistles of Peter, John, and Jude, 215.

10 Ibid.

LESSON 9

[1] Webster's New World Dictionary, Second College Ed., 889.

[2] Mounce's Complete Expository Dictionary of Old and New Testament Words, 447.

[3] "Mercy (eleos) is the love that helps the wretched, grace (charis) is the love that pardons the guilty. Mercy is placed first in order of prominence in the passage because the author means to stress our weakness in the face of his compassion and understanding. The expression in time of need, suggests the truth that there are special seasons in one's life when one has unique requirements of divine help" (Daniel H. King. Sr., The Book of Hebrews, 145).

[4] W. E. Vine, An Expository Dictionary of New Testament Words, Vol. 2, 169-170.

[5] Mounce's, op. cit., 303-304.

[6] J. I. Packer, Knowing God, 132.

[7] The grace of God will often have its conditions of reception. The walls of Jericho fell for the Israelites by the grace of God, but they had to obey God's conditions of marching around the walls (Josh. 6). Namaan was healed of leprosy by the grace of God, but not until he washed seven times in the Jordan River (2 Kgs. 5). The blind man was healed by the grace of Jesus, but only after he washed in the pool of Siloam (Jn. 9:1-11). So also Saul of Tarsus had his sins washed away, but only after being baptized (Acts 22:16). Since it is God who gives the conditions, the salvation is still by his grace. By faith, man obeys these conditions in order to access God's grace. Salvation by grace without obeying God's conditions is a false salvation.

[8] Patrick Farish, "Law and Grace," Neo-Calvinism in the Church of Christ, 118.

[9] Rienecker and Rogers, Linguistic Key to the Greek New Testament, 677.

[10] Mounce's, op. cit., 501.

[11] Ibid.

[12] C. F. Hogg and W. E. Vine, The Epistles of Paul the Apostle to the Thessalonians, 183-184.

LESSON 10

[1] Vine's Expository Dictionary of New Testament Words, Vol. 2, 165.

[2] Arthur W. Pink, The Attributes of God, www.pbministries.org/books/pink/Attributes/attrib_11.htm

[3] Funk & Wagnalls Standard Dictionary, International Ed., Vol. 1, 266.

[4] Vine's Expository Dictionary of New Testament Words, Vol. 1, 218.

[5] "Forgiveness" extended before a sinner repents is not true forgiveness, for it takes the proper action of both parties to complete a true "putting away" of sin. God does not forgive sin until the sinner repents, so we cannot rewrite the rules according to our desires. Jesus said to rebuke the sinner, and when he repents, and only then, forgive him. The rebuke must always be motivated with love for the sinner and respect for God's will, eagerly anticipating the repentance of the sinner.

[6] Jack Cottrell, What the Bible Says About God the Redeemer, 461.

[7] F. F. Bruce, The Epistle to the Hebrews, rev. ed., 375.

[8] "Since God's attitude towards sin and toward righteousness is constant, when man changes from sin to righteousness God's attitude toward that individual changes; because God is unchangeable in His attitude toward righteousness. When man changes from righteousness to sin, God's attitude toward the individual changes, because God is unchanging and thus His attitude towards sin is constant. In His nature, God cannot have the same attitude toward obedience and toward disobedience; toward

belief and unbelief. But this does not mean that an individual cannot change from the status of an unbeliever to the status of a believer" (James D. Bales, The Biblical Doctrine of God, 38).

LESSON 11

[1] J. W. McGarvey and Philip Pendleton, The Fourfold Gospel, 74.
[2] William Evans, "Wrath," The International Standard Bible Encyclopedia, Vol. 5, 3113.
[3] God's Wrath, Grace Communion International, http://www.gci.org/God/wrath
[4] James D. Bales, The Biblical Doctrine of God, 81.
[5] Relent means, "to soften in temper, resolution, etc; become less severe, stern or stubborn" (Webster's New World Dictionary, Second College Edition, 1199).
[6] Webster's New World Dictionary, Second college edition, 716.
[7] William Evans, op. cit.
[8] Covet means, "to want ardently (esp. something that another person has); long for with envy" (Webster's, op. cit. 327). It is wanting something so strongly that you are willing to do something sinful to get it.
[9] J. W. McGarvey, New Commentary on Acts of the Apostles, Vol. 1, 241.
[10] An Expository Dictionary of New Testament Words, Vol. 2, 84.

LESSON 12

[1] Webster's New Universal Unabridged Dictionary, 1556, and Gene Tope, The Providence of God, 1.
[2] W. E. Vine, Vine's Expository Dictionary of New Testament Words, Vol. 3, 227.
[3] Homer Hailey, Prayer and Providence, 114, 211.
[4] Garland Elkins, "Introduction to the Study of the Providence of God," The Providence of God, ed. Warren and Elkins, 9.
[5] Jack Cottrell, What the Bible Says About God the Ruler, 29, emphasis his.
[6] A Christian who understands these truths should never be deceived by radical environmental scenarios that predict man's destruction of the earth. Man can do temporary damage to God's natural world, but God is in control of the physical realm and man will never be able to frustrate His creative wisdom. God will not allow man to destroy the earth, for he has promised to do that at the end of time (2 Pet. 3:7, 10-12). Let us take good care of God's creation, and not be distracted by the misguided theories of those given over to atheism, false religions, and evolutionary theories.
[7] This passage is often quoted to give a positive perspective to tragic events (accidents, natural disasters, etc.) suggesting that God brings something good even out of the worst circumstances. Whether this may or may not happen, this specific passage does not teach this principle. In context, the "all things" has reference to God's eternal plan of redemption in Christ, the divine plan which works together for spiritual good for those who obey God (see Hailey, op. cit., 118-119). There are things that happen in this life that result from evil thoughts and actions that do not work for good and have very negative effects on everyone involved. This is why it is important to always "abstain from every form of evil" (1 Thess. 5:21).
[8] When we pray for the sick or for a safe journey, we must realize that God will not perform a miracle in partiality for ourselves or a loved one. There are a variety of ways God's providential care, in the physical and spiritual realm, can assist the sick and those who travel, but there is never an absolute guarantee of a recovery from illness or a safe journey because of the unpredictability of a world in which evil and suffering exist.

The faithful Christian still will glorify God with thanksgiving regardless of what may happen in this life.

[9] This also denies the false concept of karma, in which eastern religions and new age religions say that every act done will return on the doer with equal impact. While it may be true that sometimes "what goes around comes around," it is not a universal law, or force, directing the universe. Suffering can come to anyone without respect to the manner of living (Job and Jesus are examples).

[10] I have heard it happen that after the tragic death of a young person, other young people are moved to obey the gospel and prepare for death. God did not desire or cause the death of a young person in order to affect the salvation of others, but timely lessons can be learned from the most tragic of events. Those who are godly need to be ready to help others understand spiritual lessons about faith and trust in God.

[11] When someone proclaims that God "miraculously" helped them avoid tragedy and death, they need to be prepared to explain why God did not "miraculously" help someone else who suffered or died, perhaps in the very same accident or disaster. We must be very careful about saying that God was "watching out for so and so" when others might be led to think that God was not watching out for someone who fell into tragedy. For example, Peter was freed from prison (Acts 12:5-16), while James was executed (Acts 12:1-2). God watched over both apostles, and did not favor one over the other, even though one lived and one died.

[12] Cottrell, op.cit., 417.

[13] Ibid., 418.

LESSON 13

[1] "Because God did not interpose openly to punish the sins committed, the transgressor dared to imagine him to be indifferent to sin, 'such an one as himself' – no holier, no purer, no more adverse to evil...How is self-deceiving hypocrisy possible? Through false thoughts of God. Men persuade themselves that he does not mean what he says; will not be hard on them; is too indulgent really to punish sin. Not only a fatal error, but one that adds to other sins that of insulting the Most High! Terrible to think that men may set up an idol in their own thoughts – a false view of God's character and dealings..." (Pulpit Commentary, ed. H. D. M. Spence and Joseph S. Exell, Vol. 8, 387-388).

[2] Edith Hamilton, Mythology, Penguin Books, 1969, 16, 27.

[3] Webster's New World Dictionary, Second College Edition, 709.

[4] Funk & Wagnalls Standard Dictionary, International Edition, Vol. 2, 1054.

[5] Jehovah's Witnesses reason as follows: "The doctrine of a burning hell where the wicked are tortured eternally after death cannot be true, mainly for four reasons: (1) It is wholly unscriptural; (2) it is unreasonable; (3) it is contrary to God's love, and (4) it is repugnant to justice...hell, sheol or ha'des means mankind's common grave, the condition where humans, good and bad, go and rest in hope of a resurrection under God's kingdom" ("Let God Be True," Watchtower Tract and Bible Society, 1947, 99).

[6] The Pulpit Commentary, ed. H. D. M. Spence and Joseph S. Exell, Vol. 8, 387.

BIBLIOGRAPHY

Baker, D. W. "God, Names of." *Dictionary of the Old Testament: Pentateuch.* Edited by T. Desmond Alexander and David W. Baker. Downers Grove, IL: InterVarsity Press, 2003.

Bales, James D. *The Biblical Doctrine of God.* Shreveport, LA: Lambert Book House, 1974.

Baxter, Batsell Barrett. *I Believe Because...* Grand Rapids, MI: Baker Book House, 1971.

Blackmon, Luther. *God and Evolution.* Truth Tract. Bowling Green, KY: Truth Magazine Bookstore, n.d.

Bruce, F. F. *The Epistle to the Hebrews.* Revised edition. New International Commentary on the New Testament. Grand Rapids, MI: William B. Eerdmans Publishing Company, 1990.

Buswell, Jr. James Oliver. "God." *Zondervan Pictorial Bible Dictionary.* Gen. ed. Merrill C. Tenney. Grand Rapids: Zondervan Publishing House, 1967.

Carlson, Ron and Ed Decker. *Fast Facts on False Teachings.* Eugene, OR: Harvest House, 1994.

Clark, John L. and David A. Eakin. *The Theory of Evolution and Special Creation.* n. p. n.d.

Clayton, John. "New Data On 'Big Bang Theory' Putting Clinching Arguments on God's Creation," *Evidences of God.* Mentone, IN: Superior Printing, 1977.

_____. "Probability and Chance in Creation," *Evidences of God.* Mentone, IN: Superior Printing, 1977.

_____. "The Sun and Its Design." *Evidences of God,* Mentone, IN: Superior Printing, 1977.

_____. "Theistic Evolution," *Evidences of God.* Mentone, IN: Superior Printing, 1977.

Cooper, Bill, ed. *Paley's Watchmaker.* West Sussex, England: New Wine Press, 1997.

Cottrell, Jack. *What the Bible Says about God the Creator.* Joplin, MO: College Press Publishing Company, 1983.

_____. *What the Bible Says about God the Redeemer.* Joplin, MO: College Press Publishing Company, 1987.

_____. *What the Bible Says about God the Ruler.* Joplin, MO: College Press Publishing Company, 1984.

Darwin, Charles. *The Origin of Species.* ed. J. W. Burrows. New York: Penguin Books, 1968.

Davis, John J. *Moses and the Gods of Egypt: Studies in Exodus.* Second ed. Winona Lake, IN: BMH Books, 1986.

_____. *Paradise to Prison: Studies in Genesis.* Grand Rapids: Baker Book House, 1975.

Evans, William. "Love." *The International Standard Bible Encyclopedia.* James Orr, gen. ed. Grand Rapids: Wm. B. Eerdmans Publishing Co., 1939.

_____. "Wrath." *The International Standard Bible Encyclopedia.* James Orr, gen. ed. Grand Rapids: Wm. B. Eerdmans Publishing Co., 1939.

Frost, Gene. *The "Oneness" Doctrine of Pentecostalism and the Bible Doctrine of the Godhead.* A Preceptor Publication, 1974.

Funk & Wagnalls Standard Dictionary of the English Language. International Edition. Chicago: J. G. Ferguson Publishing Company, 1976.

Girdlestone, Robert B. *Synonyms of the Old Testament.* Grand Rapids: William B. Eerdmans Publishing Company, 1978.

Gish, Duane T. *Evolution: The Fossils Still Say No!* El Cajon, CA: Institute for Creation Research, 1995.

God's Wrath. Grace Communion International. http://www.gci.org/god/wrath

Hafley, Larry Ray. "The Love of God." *Guardian of Truth,* Vol. 29, No. 2, 5.

Hailey, Homer. *Prayer and Providence.* Louisville, KY: Religious Supply, Inc., 1993.

Hamilton, Edith. *Mythology.* Penguin Books, 1969.

Harkrider, Robert. *Revelation*. Bowling Green, KY: Guardian of Truth Foundation, 1997.

Hiebert, D. Edmond. "Love." *Zondervan Pictorial Bible Dictionary*. Gen. ed. Merrill C. Tenney. Grand Rapids: Zondervan Publishing House, 1967.

Hodge, Charles. *A Biblical Study of God.*

Hogg, C. F. and W. E. Vine. *The Epistles of Paul the Apostle to the Thessalonians*. Shreveport, LA: Lambert Book House, 1977.

Jenkins, Ferrell. *The Scheme of Redemption (Part 1)*. Truth in Life Workbook Series. Marion, IN: Cogdill Foundation Publications, 1974.

King, Dan. *The Days of Creation*. Bowling Green, KY: Guardian of Truth Foundation, 2001.

King, Daniel H. Sr. *The Book of Hebrews*. Truth Commentaries. Bowling Green, KY: Guardian of Truth Foundation, 2008.

_____. *The Three Epistles of John*. Truth Commentaries. Bowling Green, KY: Guardian of Truth Foundation, 2004.

Lanier, Roy H. Sr. *The Timeless Trinity for the Ceaseless Centuries*. Denver: Roy H. Lanier, Sr., 1974.

Let God Be True. Brooklyn, NY: Watchtower Bible and Tract Society, 1946.

Martin, Walter. *The Kingdom of the Cults*. Minneapolis, MN: Bethany House Publishers, 1985.

McGarvey, J. W. *New Commentary on Acts of Apostles*. Delight, AR: Gospel Light Publishing Company, n.d.

McGarvey, J. W. and Philip Y. Pendleton. *The Fourfold Gospel*. Cincinnati: Standard Publishing Co., n. d.

McKee, Aude. "How Men Come to Know God," *Guardian of Truth*, 1985 January 17, 16.

Moore, John N. *Questions and Answers on Creation/Evolution*. Grand Rapids: Baker Book House, 1976.

Morris, Henry M. *The Genesis Record*. Grand Rapids: Baker Book House, 1976.

Mounce, William D. ed. *Mounce's Complete Expository Dictionary of Old and New Testament Words*. Grand Rapids: Zondervan, 2006.

Packer, J. I. *Knowing God*. Downers Grove, IL: InterVarsity Press, 1973.

Pink, Arthur W. *The Attributes of God*, www.pbministries.org/books/pink/Attributes/attrib_11.htm

Pulpit Commentary. ed. H. D. M. Spence and Joseph S. Exell. Grand Rapids: William B. Eerdmans Publishing Co., 1962.

Rienecker, Fritz. *A Linguistic Key to the Greek New Testament*. Edited by Cleon L. Rogers, Jr. Grand Rapids, MI: Zondervan Publishing House, 1980.

Roberts, Tom. *Neo-Calvinism in the Church of Christ*. Fairmount, IN: Cogdill Foundation, 1980.

Rose, Martin. "Names of God in the OT." *The Anchor Bible Dictionary*. Edited by David Noel Freedman. Volume 4. New York: Doubleday, 1992.

Schnabel, A. O. *Has God Spoken?* San Diego: Creation-Life Publishers, 1974.

Should You Believe in the Trinity. New York: Watchtower Bible and Tract Society of New York, 1989.

Stone, Nathan. *Names of God*. Chicago: Moody Press, 1944.

Lambert, J. C. "Holiness." *The International Standard Bible Encyclopedia*. James Orr, gen. ed. Grand Rapids: Wm. B. Eerdmans Publishing Co., 1939.

Thompson, Bert. *Theistic Evolution*. Shreveport, LA: Lambert Book House, 1977.

Tope, Gene. *The Providence of God*. Bowling Green, KY: Guardian of Truth Foundation, 2000.

Trench, Richard C. *Synonyms of the New Testament*. Grand Rapids: William B. Eerdmans Publishing Company, 1980.

Turner, Allan. *The Christian & Idolatry*. Corinth, MS: Allanita Press, 2006.

Unger, Merrill F. and William White, Jr., eds. *Nelson's Expository Dictionary of the Old Testament*. Nashville: Thomas Nelson Publishers, 1980.

Vine, W. E. *Expository Dictionary of New Testament Words*. Westwood, NJ: Fleming H. Revell, 1966.

Warnock, Weldon E. "The Omnipresent God." *Guardian of Truth*, 1985 January 17, 11.

Warren, Thomas B. and Garland Elkins, eds. *The Providence of God*. Pulaski, TN: Sain Publications, n.d.

Webster's New Universal Unabridged Dictionary. Barnes & Noble Publishing, 2003.

Webster's New World Dictionary. Editor David B. Guralnik. New York: The World Publishing Company, 1972.

Whitcomb, John C. and Donald B. DeYoung. *The Moon: Its Creation, Form and Significance*. Winona Lake, IN: BMH Books, 1978.

Willis, Mike. "The Names of God." *Guardian of Truth*, 1985 January 17, 2.

Wilson, Gordon. *Theistic Evolution*. Athens, AL: The CEI Publishing Company, 1972.

Wilson, Peter. *Indestructible Foundations*. Marion, IN: Cogdill Foundation Publications, n. d.

Witherington, Bobby. "The Works of God." *Guardian of Truth*, 1985 January 17, 14.

Woods, Guy. *A Commentary on the New Testament Epistles of Peter, John, and Jude*. Nashville, TN: Gospel Advocate Company, 1983.

Woods, Tony. "The Atheist Lifestyle, Not Christianity, Is For the Weak," *The Lakeland Ledger*, 29 November 2009 (letters to the editor).

Wyatt, Robert J. "God, Names of." *The International Standard Bible Encyclopedia*. Edited by Geoffrey W. Bromiley, Revised Edition. Volume 2. Grand Rapids: William B. Eerdmans Publishing Company, 1979.

Young, Robert. *Analytical Concordance to the Bible*. New York: Funk & Wagnalls Company, n. d.